Meet the Calderwoods

Other books by William L. Coleman

Today I Feel Like a Warm Fuzzy
Animals That Show and Tell
Listen to the Animals
The Warm Hug Book

Meet the Calderwoods

Family Devotions for Children
William L. Coleman

Zondervan Publishing House
Grand Rapids, Michigan

MEET THE CALDERWOODS
Copyright © 1990 by William L. Coleman

Youth Books are published by the Zondervan Publishing House
1415 Lake Drive, S.E., Grand Rapids, Michigan 49506

Library of Congress Cataloging-in-Publication Data

Coleman, William L.
    Meet the Calderwoods : family devotions for children / William L.
Coleman.
        p.   cm.
    Summary: Presents devotional readings featuring a fictitious
family, accompanied by Biblical verses and questions for family
discussion.
    ISBN 0-310-53511-5
    1. Family—Prayer-books and devotions—English. 2. Children—
Prayer books and devotions—English. [1. Prayer books and
devotions.] I. Title.
BV255.C733   1990   90–40828
249—dc20   CIP
                                                                AC

Edited by Martha Manikas-Foster
Designed by Rachel Hostetter
Illustrated by Win Mumma

Printed in the United States of America

90 91 92 93 94 95 / DP / 10 9 8 7 6 5 4 3 2 1

Dedicated
to
Steven and Jessica

CONTENTS

The Calderwood Family

Mr. Calderwood   Mrs. Calderwood

Mark	Lisa	Andy	Sandra
Twelve years old Seventh grade	Eight years old Third grade	Seven years old Second grade	Ten years old Fifth grade
Cat: Claudia			Dog: Clyde

Get to Know the Calderwoods

If you have ever gulped down some milk and tripped over a book bag as you hurried out the door, you will understand the Calderwood family. If you have ever felt embarrassed because your sister talks too much or felt sad because your brother was sick, you know how this family feels.

Have you ever thanked God for your mother or asked God for a new car? Have you ever fed your carrots to the cat when no one was looking? If you are just an everyday person who enjoys living, I think you will have fun getting to know each of the Calderwoods and the way they handle life.

William L. Coleman
Thanksgiving Week

The Big Shoot-out

S IX BLUE, GREEN, AND ORANGE water pistols lined the steps of the back porch. One was large, shaped like a space gun. Another looked like a bear; it stood up straight and when you pushed its stomach, water shot out of its mouth. The remaining four were normal-looking and very reliable water guns.

"Pick your weapon and fill it up in one of the buckets," Mr. Calderwood announced as he adjusted his motorcycle helmet.

Each family member prepared for the great battle. Lisa had tied a piece of plastic around Claudia, the cat, to keep her dry. Clyde, the dog, rubbed against a tree. He was trying to remove the paper cup that was fastened to his head as a rain cap.

"Present arms," Mr. Calderwood directed. Everyone held the water-filled pistols high.

"On the count of three, commence firing."

The Calderwoods began fanning out in the backyard, each careful not to have his or her back exposed to anyone.

"One! Two! Three!"

Instantly the yard exploded with water. Sandra shot

her mother in the face immediately. Andy made a water Z across Mark's back. Mr. Calderwood ran for protection behind a tree while Lisa pumped three quick squirts into Clyde. Meanwhile Claudia dashed behind a bush, her eyes darting from side to side as she looked for attackers.

Mr. Calderwood tiptoed from his hiding place and took certain aim at Lisa. To his surprise, before he got a shot off, Mark and Andy soaked down the back of his head.

"No ganging up! No ganging up!" he protested between laughs.

Sandra parked herself by the garage and waited for someone to come racing around the corner. No one came. Finally impatient, she stuck her head out to see where everyone was. Squirt, squirt, squirt! Andy sprayed her face and ran away shouting.

Mrs. Calderwood got down on her knees and crawled behind the peony plants. She was able to see Mark as he walked backwards, crouched over. As she reached the end of the flowers, Mark collided with her and tumbled across her back. Their arms and legs tangled. Unable to get away, mother and son lay on the ground squirting each other, laughing uncontrollably. Tears of happiness filled their eyes and their sides ached from the joy of it all.

☐

He will yet fill your mouth with laughter and your lips with shouts of joy.
                                        JOB 8:21

☐

THE BIG SHOOT-OUT   **13**

Questions for Family Discussion

Why do you think it's fun to play games with your family?

Do you think God enjoys it when you're being silly with your family?

What kinds of new games do you think you can play with your parents?

Meet the Calderwoods

Is Too

THE DARK BLUE van left the driveway with all six of the Calderwoods tucked inside. A Saturday at Longview State Park sounded good to everyone. They could all enjoy fishing, swimming, cooking outside, and playing ball.

"Sometime I'd like to go to Piermont Park near Norwick," twelve-year-old Mark volunteered. "It's the largest park in the state."

"No it isn't," Sandra spurted. "Longview is a lot larger than Piermont."

"You're all wet," Mark shot back. "I read about it just last week."

"Well you read it wrong," Sandra said rigidly.

"Hey, you think you know everything. Piermont is larger than Longview, knucklehead."

"Is not."

"Is too."

"Is not."

"Is too."

"Let's cool it," Mrs. Calderwood jumped in. "When we get home we can all look it up together."

"Sandra always thinks she knows everything, doesn't she?" Mark insisted.

"Don't either."

"Do too."

"Don't either."

"Do too."

"Knock it off," Mrs. Calderwood demanded.

Lisa barely looked up from her book. She was glad to be sitting in the back away from the noise. Andy played with his cars, making *zoom-zoom* sounds as he raced them down his pant leg. Ignoring all the fuss, Mr. Calderwood drove on.

"What a huge barn," Mrs. Calderwood broke the silence.

"I like the dark red," Sandra said.

"It's maroon," Mark chirped.

"Dark red," Sandra growled.

"Maroon."

"Is not."

"Is too."

"Is not."

"Is too."

"How would you two like to be grounded when we get home?" Mrs. Calderwood asked sternly. "Don't make the day miserable for everyone."

The van became quiet. For the next mile or two everyone looked ahead and kept his or her thoughts private. Finally in a whisper, almost too faint to hear, came the word, "Maroon."

□

It is to a man's honor to avoid strife,
but every fool is quick to quarrel.
PROV. 20:3

Questions for Family Discussion

Was it fair for Mrs. Calderwood to be upset by Mark and Sandra's argument?

What do you think Mark and Sandra could have done to avoid quarreling?

What do you think happened when Mark said *Maroon* the final time?

What would you have done if you were Mrs. Calderwood?

The Big Cookout

WHO WANTS a second hamburger?" Mr. Calderwood called out.

He enjoyed putting on his long red apron and cooking in the backyard. The smell of a sizzling barbecue put him in great spirits.

"There's plenty of pop and chips on the table. How about you, Mark? I know you want another one."

Without waiting for a reply, Mr. Calderwood threw another meat patty on the grill and smashed it down firmly. He dashed a tad of salt across the burger like an artist adding the finishing touches to a masterpiece.

"Not too much ketchup, Lisa. You're going to ruin the taste. Good burgers don't really need any help," he announced.

Mr. Calderwood opened a second bag of potato chips and poured them into a huge plastic bowl. He hurried back to the grill, placed the well-cooked hamburger on a bun, and handed it gladly to Mark.

"Andy, ready for a second one?" Immediately he darted toward the grill but stopped suddenly. "Why, Andy, you have barely taken a bite out of the hamburger you have. Is something wrong?"

Without waiting for an answer, Mr. Calderwood took two giant steps toward Sandra.

"Take some more chips. Let me know when you want seconds."

"What's wrong with Andy?" Sandra asked.

"Why, I don't know," her father answered.

"Maybe someone should find out," said Sandra as she walked toward her younger brother.

"Are you okay?" she asked.

Andy shook his head up and down but said nothing.

"You don't look well," she continued.

Andy didn't answer.

"Does he have a fever?" Mr. Calderwood wondered.

"Who in the world did this?" Mrs. Calderwood came out of the back door holding a large, white container.

"Did what?" Mr. Calderwood asked.

"Why there were at least two dozen cookies in here and they're all gone."

"*You* ate two dozen cookies?" Sandra was startled.

Andy didn't answer.

"No wonder you can't eat your supper," Mr. Calderwood concluded.

"Son, you'll get sick if you don't eat right," said Mrs. Calderwood.

"I can't believe my brother pigged out on two dozen cookies," declared Sandra.

"Promise me you'll never do this again," Mrs. Calderwood begged.

Andy didn't answer.

THE BIG COOKOUT   **19**

☐

If you find honey, eat just enough—
too much of it, and you will vomit.

PROV. 25:16

☐

Questions for Family Discussion

Have you ever done too much of something—run around in circles or gone swinging too high—so that you became ill?

Why do you think that doing a lot of even very wonderful things can make you sick?

The Smiling Kangaroo

L ISA LINED UP her stuffed animals in the yard.

"You stand here," she told Theodore, the plump bear, as she placed him on the grass.

"And, Leonard, I'll put you over by the tree." Lisa parked her fluffy-maned lion beside the silver maple.

"Keith, you can be next to the kangaroo. A koala should get along well with a smiling kangaroo."

Lisa didn't have to put the kangaroo anywhere. Her name was Kendra and she always stood on the lawn. The Calderwoods had bought her at a flea market a couple of years ago. Kendra was a steel lawn ornament cemented into the ground. Faithfully she stood in the yard day and night, through snow or heat, season after season.

Kendra the kangaroo was brown, had a large curved tail, a pretend pouch, and a pleasant smile painted forever on her kind face. Often, when the children came home they would say "hello" to their friend who watched over the yard.

Today Lisa held a small chair in her left hand and a rope in her right. When she cracked her whiplike rope, she imagined that each of the animals would quickly obey her. Naturally Leonard the lion would growl and resist a little, but eventually each of her circus friends would fall into line.

While Lisa was busily training her collection of "wildlife," she noticed a big, older kid coming up the sidewalk. Bernie had a reputation for being a trouble-maker; as he reached the Calderwood yard, Lisa moved toward her front porch to give him plenty of room.

Neither Bernie nor Lisa spoke, but Bernie moved onto the lawn as he passed. With an evil grin the huge boy suddenly kicked Leonard the lion.

"Hey, cut that out!" Lisa protested.

Bernie drove his foot next into Keith the koala.

"Mom!" Lisa called out. "Mom!"

Undisturbed, Bernie picked up Theodore and punt-ed the bear against a tree.

"Get out of here! Mom!"

"B O N G!"

A terrible sound rang across the yard.

"You dirty ratifrat, ratifrat," Bernie mumbled to himself as he hopped around on one leg and held the big toe on his right foot.

As Mrs. Calderwood came to the door, she saw Bernie hobbling down the sidewalk talking to himself.

"What happened?" she asked Lisa.

"Nothing," she laughed back. "Bernie just learned you should never kick a smiling kangaroo."

□

Even as he walks along the road,
the fool lacks sense
and shows everyone how stupid he is.
ECCL. 10:3

Meet the Calderwoods

Questions for Family Discussion

How do you feel when somebody messes up your toys and games?

Oftentimes people who destroy our favorite things don't get punished as Bernie did. How does that make you feel?

Can you learn to forgive the people who make you angry?

Skateboard Alley

T HE TWO GIRLS hurried down the sidewalk on their skateboards. Sandra looked at ease on her yellow oversized set of wheels. Her friend, Vickie, was a bit more daring as she darted around bikes and people.

When they reached the bottom of the hill the girls made a sharp right turn into the supermarket parking lot. Skillfully they sliced their way between people and shopping carts as shoppers dashed about.

"Scuse me, Gramps," Vickie said as she cut in front of an elderly man. "Careful there, Whitey," as she raced behind an older lady.

At the far side of the parking lot Sandra and Vickie stopped to rest. Sandra picked up her skateboard and spun the wheels with her hand. Vickie nervously stood on her green skateboard, twisting back and forth.

"Did you get a look at that old girl's face?" asked Vickie. "She didn't know whether to stand still or run for her life. Come on, let's cut through again."

"I don't know," Sandra questioned, "some of these people are my neighbors."

"Big deal. What are they going to do, bite you?"

Vickie took off with Sandra close behind.

"You better get a walker," Vickie startled a woman who quickly clutched her purse. "Hey, Mom, watch those kids," as she shot between a young mother and her children.

Sandra followed behind but this time without much speed and she remained silent. Suddenly she recognized a woman from church. Spinning around she stopped next to the lady.

"Hello, Mrs. Gowen."

"Hi, Sandra. Are you shopping for your mother?"

"Not really. I just came down here to have some fun. But to tell you the truth, it isn't much fun."

"Why is that?" Mrs. Gowen asked.

"Oh, it just isn't, Mrs. Gowen. See you tomorrow in church."

Sandra pushed off on her skateboard and headed for home.

☐

Show proper respect to everyone.
1 PETER 2:17

☐

Questions for Family Discussion

Was Vickie being mean, or was she just having fun?

Why did Sandra feel bad when she saw Mrs. Gowen?

What do you do when your friends act in ways you're not comfortable with?

Meet the Calderwoods

Overhead Bars

NO PROBLEM. You can do it," Mark called out.

Mark's young brother, Andy, stood on the metal ladder rungs at the far end of the overhead bars.

"When you're ready, swing on out there. Just take one bar at a time. Go as slowly as you need to."

Andy reached out and grasped the first bar with his left hand. His seven-year-old arm barely reached.

"Great, now do it! Throw that right arm out there next to the other one and start across."

Eyes wide open and tongue sticking out the side of his mouth, Andy took the plunge. His body sank, stretching his arms to their full length. He hung in the air like old jeans on a clothesline.

"Stay calm. There are only eleven bars to go. Put your arm out to the next one. Do it. That's terrific!"

Andy thrust an arm out and grabbed the next bar. For a few seconds he was split, each arm clinging to a separate bar.

"Fantastic! Now, let go and swing that right hand over to the next bar. You can do it. Terrific!"

SMACK. Andy's right hand hurled across space

and grasped the bar. Quietly he hung, too tired to go on, his face red.

"Man, you are good at this. Ten more to go. Don't rest too long. Let's hit the next bar."

SMACK. SMACK. Slowly his hands began to slip and soon he was holding on by his fingertips.

"You can do it. Come on, sticky fingers. Pull your hands up and hold on." Mark moved closer to Andy and looked up to him.

Andy didn't speak. He wiggled each hand trying to regain a firm grip on the bar.

"That's it. You've got it. Now only nine more to go."

"What do you mean 'let's'? I'm the only one on this monster."

"Don't talk. Save your energy. Grab the next one!"

THUMP! Andy fell to the ground. He rubbed his sore hands.

"No problem, big guy," Mark reassured him. "You'll get used to sore hands. Besides it builds character."

"Easy for you to say." Andy looked at his red palms.

"Practice." Mark put his arm on Andy's shoulders and turned him toward the ladder. "The first few times I had to give up, too. But pretty soon I made it all the way across."

"Hey, I'm not going up that thing again."

"I know what you mean." Mark kept Andy walking in the direction of the bars. "I wanted to quit, too."

Still protesting, Andy lifted his leg and started climbing.

□

Encourage each other.

1 THESS. 4:18

□

Questions for Family Discussion

Did you ever want to give up trying something but later were glad you stuck with it?

Have you ever encouraged a brother, sister, or friend to keep trying something? What was that?

Do you ever think of God as a great encourager who wants us to stick with something?

A Purple Kite

THE CALDERWOOD CHILDREN enjoyed visiting their grandparents. They lived near the zoo and Talesman Park. Usually during their visit they spent an afternoon at Talesman Park riding the roller coaster and the Whirl-a-dip. It was fun being at their grandparents' home, but much more fun if they all went to the park together.

"Let's go!" Andy insisted to his dad as they stood on the porch. "I want to go on the rides." He pulled at his father's arm.

"Relax," Mr. Calderwood replied sharply. "It will take a few minutes for everyone to get ready. Just wait in the yard until everyone is together."

Andy slumped down on the porch step, folded his arms, and let his chin fall on his chest.

"Waiting is no fun. Staying in the yard is no fun. Sitting on the steps is no fun," he grumbled to himself.

Suddenly Andy's attention turned to an object in the sky. *It isn't a bird,* he thought. *Not big enough to be an airplane. It must be a kite. That's it, a purple kite! It's a beauty.*

Quickly Andy moved to the yard gate to get a

better look. The kite looked half a mile high. He wondered where it was coming from. As Andy thought about following the paper monster, he grabbed the gate with one hand. Then he remembered that his father had told him to wait in the yard.

So what? Andy told himself. *It will be hours before everybody is ready.* He pulled the gate open and started trotting in the direction of the kite.

"It can't be more than a block," Andy whispered to himself. "Just a block and I'll be right back."

He loved watching the kite bounce against the white clouds in the background. It was hopping and dancing. Darting up and then dipping. Straining upwards only to take a sudden plunge.

Jogging along, Andy soon lost track of time and distance. He crossed several streets, ran through a field, hurried past a couple of alleys.

Without warning the kite fell from the sky. Andy couldn't believe his eyes. The dancing kite had suddenly disappeared. *Well, that was fun,* Andy thought, and he began to run back to his grandparents' house.

But the second-grader didn't know where he was. He didn't know how far he had run. Andy was lost.

Andy was still wandering the streets when the sky began to grow dark. He kicked a can but without much force. From time to time he rubbed his tear-filled eyes and tried to figure out a plan. He was hungry.

"Andy! Andy!"

Not sure if he should believe his ears the young boy looked around.

"ANDY!"

Through his bleary eyes Andy saw his father jogging toward him.

"Boy, am I glad to see you," said Mr. Calderwood as he swept his son into his arms.

□

*Children, obey your parents in the Lord,
for this is right.*

EPH. 6:1

□

Questions for Family Discussion

Have you ever chased after "purple kites" and gotten lost?

Why is it a good idea to obey your parents?

Have you ever gotten into trouble because you disobeyed your parents?

The Crazy Shopping Trip

SANDRA COULD SEE Lisa at the far end of the aisle, near the dairy case. It was hard to recognize her under all those packages of food. She had stuffed a five pound sack of flour under one arm, clutched a jar of cooking oil in her right hand, and had wedged two pounds of sugar under the other elbow. Tucked tightly under her chin was a large package of chocolate chips.

"What are you doing?" Sandra called out as she came close to Lisa.

"What does it look like?" Lisa could barely open her mouth to speak because the chocolate chips held her jaw up.

"It looks like you're a vending machine. Do I put a quarter in your ear to get a prize?"

"I don't need a comedian," Lisa grumbled. "I've got to get home and bake cookies for the party."

"Give me that flour," Sandra insisted.

"Leave me alone; I can do it myself."

"You're nuts! You're going to drop everything and make a mess."

Sandra pulled at the sugar. Lisa pulled back.

"If you want to help, hand me a gallon of milk. The two percent, low fat."

Sandra picked up the plastic container.

"Slide it under my thumb," Lisa commanded.

"You can't carry this."

"I told Mom I would do it myself; so give it here!"

"Why didn't you get a shopping cart?" Sandra refused to surrender the milk.

"Because."

"Because why?"

"Because."

"Because why, Buckethead?"

"Because I thought I could carry it all and I'm going to."

"I'm going to ask Mom and Dad to have you tested to see if you're brain dead. You can't carry everything."

"Of course I can."

"Get a shopping cart."

"Get lost."

"All right. All right. Here's the milk." Sandra lodged the container under Lisa's thumb. "How about a few more things?" Sandra grabbed a ring of garlic and adjusted it securely on Lisa's head. Quickly she laid a pack of cheese on Lisa's left shoulder. Automatically Lisa shifted her head to hold the new package in place.

"I'm calling the manager," Lisa mumbled.

"Go ahead, call the manager; he should get a good laugh. Tell him you are Zelda the Wonderwoman and you never let anyone help you."

□

Cast all your anxiety on him because he cares for you.

1 PETER 5:7

□

Questions for Family Discussion

Lisa was taking care of an errand the way she told her mom that she would. Is there really anything wrong with the way Lisa was shopping?

Why is it hard to ask others for help when we need it?

How can we give our anxieties—our concerns and troubles—to God? Why would he want us to?

Ticked Off

HOW'D THE VOLLEYBALL game go?"
Lonnie asked Mark as they arrived at the picnic table.
"Let me pour some ice tea for you."

Lonnie was Mark's Sunday school teacher and
they got along well.

"The game was all right, but let me tell you something, I really hate that Brad." Mark's hand shook as he
accepted the paper cup filled with tea.

"Hate's pretty strong." Lonnie poured a cup for
himself.

"I can't help it. The guy's always on my case."

"He's a little pushy," Lonnie admitted.

"A little? He bugs me to death. Anytime I mess
up he teases me. I can't say anything right. He always
jumps in and makes fun of what I say."

"I don't think you're the only one. It might just be
his personality."

"That's no excuse. There's no excuse for being
mean." Mark picked up a handful of potato chips.
"That's why I hate him."

"You want me to talk to him?" Lonnie asked.

"No, I'm just a big cry baby. I'm sorry I said anything."

"But that's how you really do feel. There's nothing wrong with saying how you feel."

"I just hate him." Mark spit out his words.

"If you decide to hate Brad, that's going to take a lot of work."

"Oh, no! It's easy for me to hate Brad."

"It would be hard work for me to hate someone." Lonnie reached for a brownie. "When I hate someone I can feel my heart pounding faster. My face feels hot and sometimes my stomach grinds. Hating someone just wears me out."

"But sometimes you just can't help it."

"I suppose. But hate stops me from thinking about good things. I have to spend too much of my time trying to remember to hate that person. And then I have to remember why I hate him. Can you believe that once I hated someone and I couldn't remember why I hated him? Hate is a tricky business."

"You can't just ignore someone when he treats you like trash."

"I suppose. But sometimes a sense of humor helps."

"I can't laugh all the time when I get kicked around."

"Probably not, but a few laughs might help. Tell you what I'll do. Why don't we spend some time in our Sunday school class discussing how we treat each other?"

"Hey, don't do it for me. I can take care of it myself. That jerk doesn't bother me."

"Yeah, I can tell; you're handling it real well."

TICKED OFF **37**

□

If anyone says, "I love God," yet hates his brother, he is a liar. For anyone who does not love his brother, whom he has seen, cannot love God, whom he has not seen. And he has given us this command: Whoever loves God must also love his brother.

1 JOHN 4:20–21

□

Questions for Family Discussion

Do you think it is really all that bad to hate someone?

Why would you be a liar if you say that you love God and also hate another person?

How is loving the mean girl in school or the bully down the block connected to loving God?

Meet the Calderwoods

Everybody Blushed

NDY, COME WITH ME for just a minute. We'll be right back."

Andy's aunt, uncle, and grandparents were visiting for the afternoon on their way to a ball game. Mr. Calderwood and his son left them for a moment and moved toward the back door.

"I don't understand it," said Andy as they walked toward the back fence. "Nobody laughed at my joke."

"No, in fact everyone was pretty shocked. Where did you hear that?"

"At school. Everybody at recess laughed at it," Andy said puzzled.

"Who told it to you?"

"Tom did. He gets lots of funny jokes."

"Do you know what the joke is about? Sit down for a sec." Mr. Calderwood rearranged two lawn chairs.

"Not really, but it's funny."

"The joke is about sex."

"Well, I kind of knew that."

"There's nothing wrong with sex. God created sex for married couples. But when we make jokes about sex, we make a lot of people feel embarrassed, like you just did."

"Why?"

"I think it's because sex is personal and private. It's meant for two married people in love. Sex wasn't meant to be written on walls or drawn on sidewalks. Sex is too important for that."

"But I hear adults tell jokes about sex."

"Sure you do. And it's a tricky business. Some jokes are okay. But other jokes are ugly and come out dirty."

"How am I supposed to know the difference?"

"It is hard to know. Some jokes just go too far and you have to know what not to joke about."

"I'm really confused now."

"It is confusing. But for now, do this. If you think the joke is dirty or has to do with sex, don't tell it. And if you aren't sure, try it out on me. I'll tell you right away if it is dirty or not."

Andy jumped off his chair as his father stood up.

"This growing up is really weird," Andy said.

"Sometimes it really is, son. It really is."

□

Nor should there be obscenity, foolish talk or coarse joking, which are out of place, but rather thanksgiving.

EPH. 5:4

□

Questions for Family Discussion

Why is it a bad idea to repeat words or jokes you don't understand?

Do you have questions about sex that your parents could answer?

Is there any word that you have heard your parents use that you would like to have them explain to you?

Chewing Gum in the Chair

LISA REACHED DOWN beside the cushion where she was sitting. The large, green, overstuffed chair was famous for swallowing coins, toy cars, and barrettes. Now it had opened up and taken the chewing gum that had fallen from her mouth.

As Lisa groped under the cushion her finger jabbed into something wet and gooey. Cautiously she pulled up her hand to see a long string of ugly soft gum, most of which was stuck, like wet glue, inside the chair.

While her parents watched television, Lisa shoved her sticky hand back into the chair and took time to think. After several minutes of careful thought, she pulled up her hand and announced with obvious disgust: "Look what Clyde did."

"What did that dog do now?" asked Mrs. Calderwood.

"He was chewing gum and spit it down here," Lisa explained as she stood up.

"Clyde was chewing gum?" Mr. Calderwood said bewildered.

"Sounds crazy," Lisa added, "but sometimes he does."

"Dogs don't normally chew gum." Mrs. Calderwood took a tissue and began to clean off Lisa's fingers.

"I told you it sounds crazy."

"Weren't you chewing gum just a few minutes ago?" Mr. Calderwood asked.

"Well, yeah, but I swallowed mine."

"Are you positive?" Mrs. Calderwood pressed the question.

". . . Probably."

"You weren't trying to lie your way out of it by blaming poor Clyde, were you?" Mrs. Calderwood wondered.

"No. No. I must have been kidding about Clyde. Sure, I was chewing the gum and then I was kidding about Clyde."

"There's a big difference between lying and kidding," Mr. Calderwood insisted.

"I know, I know," Lisa said nervously.

"Kidding can be fun, but lying is wrong," Mr. Calderwood went on.

"Hey, I know that. Can't you guys take a joke?"

☐

Do not lie to each other.

COL. 3:9

☐

Questions for Family Discussion

What are the advantages of lying?

What are the advantages of telling the truth?

The Bible tells us that we should tell the truth because Christians have been re-created in the image of God, and lying is not part of that image. What are other ways in which we can behave that will please God?

A Rickety Pier

HOLD IT BY both claws," Mr. Calderwood called out to Andy. "That makes a better picture."

Andy stretched the crab to its full width.

"Let's get Lisa over here with her crab now." Mr. Calderwood advanced the film in his camera. "Sandra, don't go out on the pier. You know the man told us to stay off."

"Hold it higher, Lisa. You could try smiling," Mr. Calderwood kidded. "You want everyone to know you had a good vacation, don't you?"

Snap.

"That's a good shot," Mr. Calderwood declared.

"How about my turtle shell?" Mark asked.

"Sure," his father replied. "Sandra, do you want me to come out on the pier and get you? Come off the pier—immediately!"

"Do you think I should show the back of the shell or the belly?" Mark wondered.

"Why not both. I've got enough film. Sandra!" Mr. Calderwood yelled, "turn around and come off the pier now."

Sandra stopped, turned, and gave her father an incredibly dirty look.

"I can't do anything," she growled.

"Great, now let's see the other side of the shell."

CRASH! PLUNK!

"Sandra!" Mrs. Calderwood shouted.

Sandra was sprawled on the dock with one leg dangling through the broken wood.

"Hold on! We'll be right there," Mrs. Calderwood reassured Sandra.

"Ouch! Ouch!" Sandra screamed. "A crab bit me. Hurry!"

Mrs. Calderwood tiptoed across the pier.

"Ouch! Ouch!" Sandra repeated.

Her mother helped the crying girl free her leg by pulling it back through the shattered board. Sandra's leg was scratched, but she grabbed first for her bitten toes.

"You didn't even come to help me," Sandra complained to her father who still stood on the beach. "You don't care what happens to me."

"Sure I do. That's why I told you to stay off the pier. Try to hold that shell straight, Mark."

□

Whoever loves discipline loves knowledge,
but he who hates correction is stupid.
                                    PROV. 12:1

□

Questions for Family Discussion

Why do you think the Bible says that it is wise to pay attention when we're corrected?

How can we love discipline?

13

The Shark Sucker

Look WHAT'S over here." Mr. Calderwood beckoned his son.

"They are a neat black." Mark joined his father in front of the huge aquarium. A three foot, slender fish remained motionless in the water.

"It's a shark sucker; they attach themselves to the bottom of sharks and take free rides. I saw some when I was in Florida."

"How do they hold on?" Mark wondered.

"Do you see that flat area on top of its head?"

"Yeah."

"That's really like a suction cup. They come up under a shark and sort of paste themselves under the shark's chin. Wherever the shark goes, the sucker rides along."

"Can it get off?"

"No problem. By moving forward they can let go whenever they want to, but why should they? It's a free ride and they don't have to swim or make decisions or anything."

"I bet nothing bothers them either, being that close to a shark's mouth," Mark added.

"The shark even takes care of the sucker's food. When the shark eats, bits of flesh drop from its mouth and this little freeloader catches them. You can't get much lazier than that."

"That would be the life," Mark decided. "You don't have to work; you don't worry; you just let the big shark take care of everything."

"It works better for fish than it does for people. For instance, drug addicts try it all the time. They figure that if they can get some drugs, they don't have to worry about anything." Mr. Calderwood turned serious.

"Sure, but if they want to, they can just give up the drugs like the fish cuts loose from the shark."

"They wish. They let drugs run their lives and soon they can't take control back again."

"Well, sometimes."

"Too often," Mr. Calderwood said as he shook his head. "No thanks, I don't want a shark controlling me and I don't want some goofy drug controlling me either."

"How did we get so serious?" Mark asked.

"I don't know. Let's check out the turtles."

☐

It is God's will that . . . each of you should learn to control his own body in a way that is holy and honorable, not in passionate lust like the heathen, who do not know God.

1 THESS. 4:3–5

☐

THE SHARK SUCKER   **49**

Questions for Family Discussion

What things, like drugs, can control you so that you can't make your own decisions anymore?

How can you avoid such things?

Do you have a plan for how to avoid drugs when they are offered to you?

14

The Rubber Band Plane

ANDY TURNED the stick in the tail of the plane, twisting the rubber band tightly. With his other hand he held the propeller in place and readied his craft for its flight.

The tree house was Andy's favorite place from which to launch airplanes. In the past, Andy's other planes had soared across the backyard and landed in the grass near Mr. Ralston's garage.

When the rubber band was taut, Andy held the plane high above his head and let go of the wooden toy. The aircraft took a quick lunge upward, stopped for a second in mid-air and plunged propeller first toward the ground.

"Rats!" Andy exclaimed as he started his climb down to retrieve the plane.

Much to his surprise the plane had survived the crash in remarkably good condition. The wings were pushed back and slanted but without any permanent damage. Even though the propeller was bent slightly, Andy was sure the plane would fly again.

The second-grader pulled his strength together and forced his way back up the huge tree with its robust trunk and spreading limbs. When Andy arrived back at the tree house, he rewound the rubber band until it was tight. With renewed enthusiasm he tossed the plane back out into space.

Stubbornly the craft leaped into the air head first and then hung above the ground while the propeller spun around with all its strength.

"Go!" Andy shouted. "Go!"

The plane appeared to try but somehow couldn't manage to hold itself in place. Sadly, it dipped its nose and fell helplessly to earth.

"Rats!" Andy grumbled all the way to the ground.

"What's wrong?" Mark asked Andy as he picked up his plane.

"I don't know. The goofy thing just wants to crash."

"What did you do with the package it came in?" Mark took the plane and looked closely.

"I threw it away."

"Well, maybe you want to go look for it."

"Why?" Andy took his plane back.

"I think if you look at the instructions on the package you'll see you put the wings in upside down."

"Upside down?"

"Check the instructions, space man; you can save yourself a lot of headaches."

□

He who obeys instructions guards his soul.
PROV. 19:16

□

Questions for Family Discussion

Why is it important to follow directions?

How can following directions make life easier for us? How can it guard our lives?

THE RUBBER BAND PLANE

Sandra's Team Wins

A FIFTH GRADE GIRL crashed her bat into the softball and began running to first base. The ball sailed over the shortstop's head while another base runner dashed home from third base.

"We win! We win!" Denise leaped into the air and then hugged Sandra, her teammate.

"Great! Fantastic! Thank God!" Sandra was just as excited.

When the celebration finally died down and both teams headed for their cars, Denise caught up with Sandra again.

"You don't mind if I ask you something?" Denise forced the words out.

"Of course not."

"Well, I know you are sort of religious, but what you said back there . . . ."

"Back there?"

"Yeah, you know, about thanking God."

"No big deal," Sandra said. "I say it a lot."

"But," Denise ventured, "it was only a ball game."

"Absolutely."

"And winning a ball game isn't, uh, exactly a miracle or anything," Denise said.

"Of course not."

"And God didn't pick our team to win or anything like that—right?"

"Probably not." Sandra smiled.

"Well, if God didn't have anything to do with the game, and God doesn't care who won it, why did you thank God?"

"I didn't say God didn't have anything to do with the game. I have no way of knowing. But I don't have to know. God is good to us all the time so I just like to thank him."

"You like to thank him?" Denise scratched her head.

"Sure, I don't have to thank God. It isn't a law or something."

"Then why do you do it?"

"Maybe because God does so many great things. Some of them I don't even see. So I thank God just for being God."

□

He gave thanks and broke the loaves.
MATT. 14:19

□

Questions for Family Discussion

The verse at the end of the story is about Jesus Christ and how even he thanked God. How is it helpful to know that Jesus enjoyed thanking his father?

How might thanking God embarrass you in front of your friends? How might you learn to not let that hurt your feelings?

Do you think you could find something to thank God for even when you lose a ball game or don't receive what you've asked for?

The Possum Mother

Q UICK, QUICK!" Andy came running to his father.

"There's a hawk in the woods! It's trying to attack the baby possums. Hurry!"

"Coming!" Mr. Calderwood picked up a garden hoe and ran with his son to the wooded area behind their home.

"He's going to carry them off! Run!" Andy raced through the small meadow.

"I'll be there!" his father yelled.

"I chased the hawk off twice but it keeps coming back," Andy explained breathlessly. "I don't know where the mama possum is. The babies will be gone for sure."

They reached the trees and soon could see the hawk on the ground. Wings spread wide, the bird danced around on its taloned feet making frightening sounds.

"Get! Get!" Mr. Calderwood shouted.

As they came into clear view of the pending attack, Andy yelled, "It's the mother! The possum mother came back."

Sharp teeth showing, the adult opossum hissed at

the menacing bird. Shaking, the four babies tried to hide behind their mother.

The approach of Andy and his father seemed too much for the hawk and suddenly it flew away.

"We made it, Dad. Just in time!"

While they looked on, each of the tiny opossums climbed up on the mother's back and seemed to snuggle into her fur. Unhurriedly the large female walked away with her important cargo safely aboard.

"Their mother sure knows how to do it. I kept calling to the babies but they wouldn't come to me." Andy thrust his hands on his hips as he and his father started home.

"That's because you aren't a possum. They couldn't understand you. For all they knew, you were just another enemy."

"It sure was frustrating, trying to help."

"No doubt about it." Mr. Calderwood pushed back some branches as they walked. "I suppose that's why Jesus Christ came down and became a human being. When he became one of us—spoke our language and all—we found it easier to follow him."

"I'm glad he didn't come as a hawk or a possum; I'd really be confused."

□

Who, being in very nature God,
did not consider equality with God some-
thing to be grasped,
but made himself nothing,
taking the very nature of a servant,
being made in human likeness.

PHIL. 2:6–7

Questions for Family Discussion

Why do you think Jesus Christ became a human?

Even though Christ became a human and used our language, do you think he's sometimes hard to understand? What could you do to make it easier to understand him?

Do you think Jesus ever had disagreements with his parents when he was a child? What would they have been about?

17

Sacking In

RISE AND SHINE!" Mrs. Calderwood put up the shade in Sandra's bedroom and allowed the sunlight to flood in. "It's almost ten o'clock. You promised to help me paint the bathroom cabinet this morning."

"H'm" was all Sandra managed to reply. She reburied her head in the pillow.

"Looks like you stayed up for the Midnight Madness movie. What was it last night? *Search for the Sizzling Sea Serpent?*" Mrs. Calderwood chuckled to herself.

Sandra showed only minimal signs of life.

"Come on. Up, up, up!" Taking Sandra by the shoulders, her mother wrestled the limp girl to a sitting position. Immediately Sandra tumbled sideways back onto the bed.

"Lady, I'm ready to go and you're still a zombie. Throw on some paint duds and let's get moving." She again propped up the human sack. Sandra's head fell into her hands.

Mrs. Calderwood walked to the bedroom door.

"And sometime today get the oil can out of the garage and give these hinges a small squirt; the squeak is driving me bonkers. I'll be right back to check on you." Mrs. Calderwood left the room, pushing the noisy door behind her.

Within five minutes Sandra's mother returned and abruptly opened the bedroom door.

"Are you dressed yet?"

She didn't see Sandra on the bed. She looked toward the closet. No sign there.

"Sandra," she said with exasperation to the large bundle piled on the floor. "Is this all the farther you made it? Get up."

Mrs. Calderwood forced the wiggly body to its feet and held her in place.

"Tonight you're to be in bed at 9:00, and if you're not in the kitchen in ten minutes, we'll make that 8:00."

Mrs. Calderwood walked away briskly and stopped at the door.

"And don't forget to oil these hinges."

☐

As a door turns on its hinges.
so a sluggard turns on his bed.
                                        PROV. 26:14

☐

Questions for Family Discussion

Do you think you are a lazy person or do you have lots of energy?

Sometimes do you pretend to be lazy to get out of work?

18

He Hit Me!

M OM! MOM!"

Sandra hurried into the backyard crying. Her mother was kneeling by the peonies but stood up when she saw her daughter in pain.

"He hit me, Mom. That dirty rat hit me."

"Who hit you?" Mrs. Calderwood put her arms around Sandra.

"Mark! Who else? He's got a terrible temper."

"Why would your brother hit you?"

No sooner had she asked this than Mark came out of the back door huffing and puffing. He walked a straight line toward his sister and mother.

"Did she tell you what she did?" Mark bellowed.

"Hold on, both of you." Mrs. Calderwood put down her clippers and pulled off her rubber gloves. "Let Sandra talk first."

"Mark hit me. Like a little baby, he hit. Look!" She shifted her shoulder to show a sizable red welt on the back of her arm.

"You did this?" Mrs. Calderwood asked.

"Oh, now I'm the criminal. Did she tell you why I

hit her? Did she tell you she took my tapes and didn't even ask?"

"You hit her for taking your tapes?"

"Sure. Defend her. But if she kept taking your stuff, you'd be pretty mad, too."

"I didn't take the tapes; I borrowed them. He borrows my tapes all of the time. Don't you?"

"I ask."

"All right. All right. Sandra, go to your room and wait for me. Mark, you stay here," Mrs. Calderwood directed.

"I knew I'd get blamed for this; I always get blamed," Mark complained.

"It sounds to me like both of you are to blame," said Mrs. Calderwood.

"Sure," Mark said sarcastically.

"Sandra has no right to take your tapes, I admit that; but you have no business hitting her."

"Sometimes you just have to."

"Not really. When I disagree with the clerk at the store or I have an argument at work, I don't hit someone."

"I can't help it. When you've had it, you've had it."

"Believe me, Mark," she put her hands on Mark's elbows, "I know how you feel, but I also know I have to control myself."

"I couldn't help it."

"It's hard, but you have to control yourself. When you lose your temper like that, someone could get hurt. If you refuse to let evil run your life, you can keep your cool. Now I have to talk to your sister about those tapes."

□

Submit yourselves, then, to God. Resist the devil, and he will flee from you."

JAMES 4:7

□

Questions for Family Discussion

What things make you really angry?

How do you think you can resist the devil and keep your cool?

Do you ever lose your temper and break things? Why do you or why don't you lose your temper?

19

Crossing the Stream

WHENEVER THE CLOUDS covered the sun the valley became cool and Andy moved closer to the campfire. He and his dad had stayed at the campsite while the rest of the family drove to town for supplies.

"We can toast marshmallows until the family gets back." Mr. Calderwood whittled his stick to a point and handed it to Andy.

Andy zipped the front of his jacket, then slipped a marshmallow over the stick and held it over the flames. He liked his black with a crust that crinkled when he bit into it.

"Dad, what's it like to die?"

Mr. Calderwood couldn't believe his ears. He was looking forward to all kinds of questions about bears, birds, even mountain lions. It didn't seem like the time or place to bring up death.

"Kevin's grandfather died and I wondered what it must be like to die. Do you just stop breathing? Does it hurt? I wondered if Kevin's grandfather could still think."

"That's a tough one," Mr. Calderwood thought out loud.

"Do you think he knew his family was standing beside the coffin? That was creepy," said Andy.

"I've never died," Mr. Calderwood said to try to lighten up the conversation. "But let's try this. Do you remember a few years ago when we came up here to camp and we climbed Mt. Princeton? You were little then."

Andy nodded his head while he ate another burned marshmallow.

"We came to that large stream with the rushing water," Mr. Calderwood continued. "It was too deep and fast for you to cross. So I picked you up in my arms and you closed your eyes and I carried you over the stream. When you opened your eyes you were safely on the other side. Remember?"

Andy remained silent.

"I think that's what death must be like. We close our eyes on this side of the stream and when we open them we find that Jesus Christ has carried us in his arms over to the other side."

"H'm," said Andy.

☐

The eternal God is your refuge,
and underneath are the everlasting arms.
DEUT. 33:27

☐

Questions for Family Discussion

Has someone you loved died? How did it make you feel?

What questions do you have about death and whom do you know who could help you talk about them?

20

Walking the Tree

HOLD UP! Hold up!" Mrs. Calderwood yelled to Lisa. "I've got to rest."

"Are you getting soft or what?" Lisa walked back down the trail to join her mother. Mrs. Calderwood was leaning against a huge rock. She stretched her back across the flat surface; it made a perfect recliner.

"I don't think I ever was too great at running up and down mountains," she said as she gasped for breath.

"Let's cross here. Over that neat fallen tree," said Lisa energetically.

"Don't even think about it." Mrs. Calderwood took a quick look. "That must be a fifteen foot drop into the crevice."

"Come on, Mom. You don't want to be a chicken."

"Chicken, nothing. There's no telling what that trunk might do. What if it rolls and dumps you off?"

"What if. What if," mocked Lisa.

"Laugh if you want, but it may be rotten and could just fall apart with you on top, little lady."

"What if. What if," Lisa went on. "It's called faith;

remember, Mom? You have to believe. That's what you said."

Lisa walked over to the trunk and bounced up on the end.

"LISA, be careful. Those branches could break off."

"No, it's the same thing. I have to believe the tree will hold me. One step at a time. Just like being a Christian."

"I'm not watching." Mrs. Calderwood put her hand over her eyes.

"Don't be chicken." Lisa moved out to the middle of the trunk, grabbing branches as she walked.

"A-A-A-A-A-A-H!" Lisa screamed.

"No problem," Lisa added, weakly. "Just a wet spot. The branches held. Piece of cake." She struggled to her feet.

"Get off of there!" Mrs. Calderwood demanded.

"Okay, okay. But I believed and the tree held me."

☐

And without faith it is impossible to please God, because anyone who comes to him must believe that he exists and that he rewards those who earnestly seek him."
HEB. 11:6

☐

Questions for Family Discussion

Do you ever have trouble believing in God when you can't see Him?

Have you ever helped someone because you believed God wanted you to help that person?

WALKING THE TREE

The Secret Bag

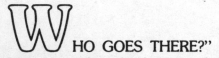HO GOES THERE?"

Lisa stopped at the bottom of the stairs when she heard her mother's voice.

"What are you doing up this early? It isn't even light outside," Mrs. Calderwood asked from the kitchen.

"I just have some errands to run," Lisa answered shyly.

"Errands? What are you doing, delivering milk? Nobody is up at this hour."

"That's why I have to do it now. I don't want anyone to see me." Lisa reached for her jacket.

"This is really weird. What's in the bag?"

"I have a good idea, Mom. Why don't you go back and make the cereal while I deliver this little package and we can both forget it."

"The bag," Mrs. Calderwood demanded as she held out her hand.

Lisa tightened her lips as she surrendered the package. "This is strictly private."

"It has Topan's name on it. The Laotian girl. Your new jeans? What in the world is going on?"

"Just let me do my thing," Lisa begged. "I let you put anything in your bags."

"Now that's a big-hearted daughter."

"Please! They will soon be up and I don't want them to catch me."

"But you have only a few pairs of jeans," her mother reminded Lisa. "Don't think I'm going to replace these."

"I understand." Lisa put her red jacket on and pulled up the hood.

"Well, I've got to go to work today. I can't stand here all morning." Mrs. Calderwood returned the bag.

"Thanks, Mom."

Lisa moved quickly toward the door, unlocked it, and left.

BANG! The door slammed shut.

Slowly the door reopened and Lisa's hooded head poked inside.

"Sorry," she whispered.

"Will you get!" Mrs. Calderwood smiled.

☐

The Lord Jesus himself said: "It is more blessed to give than to receive."
ACTS 20:35

☐

THE SECRET BAG

Questions for Family Discussion

Can you think of ways you might give to others? You don't have to give away your clothing; you could commit your time to helping an older neighbor plant a garden, or shovel the sidewalk.

Meet the Calderwoods

22

Porky and Fred

Ｓ ANDRA SET her two best stuffed friends on the coffee table in the living room.

"Don't Porky and Fred look sad?" she asked her mother.

"I hadn't really noticed." Mrs. Calderwood barely looked up from her sewing needle and the clothes she was mending.

"Well, look closer then. Porky's eyes are sunk low on her little pig cheeks. And Fred's dog jaws are dropping. You can see that."

"Not quite, but if you say so."

"You can tell things like that when you spend a lot of time with them."

"I have a feeling this conversation is going somewhere, but I don't know where yet."

"It's loneliness, Mom. That's what it is, loneliness."

"Porky and Fred are lonely?" Mrs. Calderwood reached over and took a sip of coffee.

"They need company."

"I can see that," Mrs. Calderwood replied dryly.

"Particularly they need the company of Andy the Panda."

PORKY AND FRED   **75**

"Oh, Andy the Panda?"

"You've seen Linda's stuffed panda; she brought it over lots of times." Sandra moved Porky and Fred farther apart. "It has soft fur and those large black eyes. Linda has all kinds of stuffed animals."

"And that's why Porky and Fred need a panda? Because Linda has one?" her mother asked.

"It isn't just that. You see them in all the stores and catalogs and soon everyone will have a panda."

"Why, I wouldn't want one just because everyone else had one," Mrs. Calderwood added.

"No, you wouldn't, but you're ol- ol- I mean, not young. You don't understand."

"I may not." Mrs. Calderwood put her mending down. "But I do know this; that when I want what everyone else has, I'll soon start to go nuts."

"But you and Dad have chairs and lamps because everyone else has them, don't you?"

"There is some truth to that." Mrs. Calderwood left her chair and joined Sandra on the floor. "But I have to be careful that I don't want everything everyone else has."

"I don't either." Sandra grew impatient. "But things like pandas are important. You don't want everyone to think I am left out, do you?"

"No, but I guess I don't want everyone else to run your life and mine."

"I knew you wouldn't understand." Sandra abruptly stood, knocked Porky and Fred to the floor and stomped into her bedroom.

□

A heart at peace gives life to the body,
but envy rots the bones.

PROV. 14:30

□

Questions for Family Discussion

Is there anything really wrong with wanting to have what other people have?

What is envy?

How do you feel when you want something but aren't allowed to get it?

23

Let's Go Skating

MARK, MARK!" Larry was calling from across the street. He and Jeff dodged cars as they jogged through traffic. "Wait up!"

"What's happening?" Mark asked as his friends hopped up on the curb.

"Let's go skating tonight. My dad's giving us a ride," said Larry.

"Hey, I'd like to. How about tomorrow night?" Mark asked.

"Mark, read my lips. My dad's going to give a ride tonight, not tomorrow night."

"You guys know I would like to go, but I can't."

"Don't tell us you are going to study," Jeff ridiculed him.

"No, not this time. My youth group meets tonight."

"You mean you still go to that church group? Come on, that's for kids," Larry complained. "Does your mom make you go to that?"

"Not really; she never said. I just like to go," Mark explained.

"You think the guys in youth group are better than us, don't you?" Jeff whined.

"Give me a break," Mark begged. "I do lots of things with you guys. This is just the wrong night."

"Youth group can't be that much fun," said Larry. "You're after a girl, aren't you? Kathy Palmberg goes to youth group, doesn't she?"

"Sure she does, but that's not the whole reason."

"See, you're just like the rest of us, Mark, baby." Jeff pointed his finger at Mark's chest. "You go where the girls are. That's where it's at."

"Kathy Palmberg is okay, too, but there's more to it than that."

"Like what?" Larry spread his legs and faced Mark squarely. "What else? Cookies, punch, you play games, what's the big deal?"

"You asked for it, remember that." Mark hesitated. "I go to learn about Jesus Christ."

"Uh, oh!" Jeff stretched his fingers out in magic fashion. "That heavy spirit stuff."

"Look you asked me and I told you." Mark started to walk away. "I don't expect you to understand."

"Don't go off the deep end and get spooky on us, Mark." Larry began to move in the other direction.

"It isn't that," Mark protested.

"When you see Jesus, tell him we want him to go skating with us," Jeff shouted as he hustled back across the busy street.

☐

Blessed are you when people insult you, persecute you and falsely say all kinds of evil against you because of me. Rejoice and be glad, because great is your reward

in heaven, for in the same way they perse-
cuted the prophets who were before you.
MATT. 5:11–12

☐

Questions for Family Discussion

Has anyone ever made fun of you because you are a Christian or because you go to church? How did you answer him?

How do your friends know you are a Christian? What is Christian about your life?

An Apple a Day

WANT TO PLAY CATCH?"

Mr. Calderwood came out the back door with two gloves and a shiny white hardball.

"Sure!" Andy stood up from his perch on the cement steps. Quickly, he took one more bite out of his apple and tossed the skinny core into the trash barrel.

Mr. Calderwood jogged halfway across the backyard and threw the ball to his son. Andy barely got his glove on in time. He threw the ball back and it smacked loudly in his father's glove.

"That apple looked pretty good," said Mr. Calderwood. "You don't have an extra one, do you?"

Thump! The ball pounded into Andy's mitt.

"No problem," Andy insisted. "I've got a couple more."

Swish! He fired a pitch back to his dad.

"Apples are good for you, you know." Mr. Calderwood twisted his fingers on the ball and delivered a knuckleball.

"Whatever." Andy backhanded his catch and sent the ball whistling back.

"You had a couple of apples yesterday, didn't

you?" Mr. Calderwood held the ball and waited for an answer.

"I suppose. It's hard to remember."

"Maybe an apple or two the day before?" His father attempted a curve ball.

"I don't spend my time counting apples, Dad."

"I don't usually either. Has someone been giving you those apples? We don't have any here at the house." Mr. Calderwood threw a ground ball to his son.

"Well, kind of." Andy dropped the grounder.

"I hope someone has been giving them to you because Mr. Worthy says some boys are climbing the fence and stealing apples out of his tree." Mr. Calderwood held the ball.

"Not me, Dad, honest."

"Then where do you get the apples?"

"A friend gives them to me."

"Who?"

"I don't know if I should say now."

"Son, be smart. Don't take any more apples from anyone. And don't get messed up in stealing apples."

"It wasn't me, Dad."

"Eating stolen apples is almost the same. No more apples."

Smack! Mr. Calderwood's fastball ripped into Andy's glove.

□

For you know that we dealt with each of you as a father deals with his own children, encouraging, comforting and urging you to live lives worthy of God, who calls you into his kingdom and glory.
1 THESS. 2:11–12

□

Questions for Family Discussion

Do your parents ever warn you to stay out of trouble? How does that make you feel?

Have you ever been glad that they gave you advice?

25

No Dumb Kids

Y OU GO AHEAD and climb with everyone else," Mr. Calderwood told Lisa. "I better tend this fire until it burns down some more. Then I'll douse it with water."

"I'd rather wait for you." Lisa sat down on the picnic bench.

"If you want to keep Colorado beautiful, you have to keep an eye on these fires." Mr. Calderwood spread the burning sticks apart. "The forests can burn in a hurry."

"Did you find college tough?" Lisa asked. "Ashley Perkins just graduated and she told me it was hard."

"It wasn't too bad." Lisa's father sat down next to her. "But I almost didn't go."

"Why not?"

"For a long time I thought I wasn't smart enough. My grades weren't bad; it was just how I felt about myself." He tossed dry leaves on the lingering flames.

"You seem real smart to me," said Lisa, swinging her feet under the bench.

"I do all right; but something always bothered me. When I was about your age, I knocked over our neighbor's trash cans. I was just goofing off. Well, the old guy next door came running out and grabbed me."

"Bet you were scared."

"I was shaking like a blender. He was holding my arm and yelling at me and then he said, 'You're just a dumb kid.' Man, did he look mean."

"You didn't let that bother you, did you?"

"Not at first. But I was surprised how it bothered me later. If I did badly on a test, I would remember what that old guy said. If I dropped something, I would hear him screaming at me again."

"You don't let it bother you now, do you?"

"Not much, but when it came time to apply for college, I was really scared. I didn't know if I could make it and the neighbor's words kept coming back."

"Wow, that's terrible."

"In some ways, sure, but remembering it also makes me careful what I say to others, especially children. I know that a few words can really tear you up."

Mr. Calderwood picked up a bucket and dumped water on the sizzling coals.

☐

Consider what a great forest is set on fire by a small spark. The tongue also is a fire, a world of evil among the parts of the body. It corrupts the whole person, sets the whole course of his life on fire, and is itself set on fire by hell.
                                        JAMES 3:5–6

☐

NO DUMB KIDS   **85**

Questions for Family Discussion

Has anyone called you a name and hurt your feelings? Does it still bother you?

Do you sometimes call people ugly names without thinking?

Have you ever felt like you were dumb or ugly or weird because of something someone said? Would you like to tell your parents or a teacher about the remark that hurt your feelings?

26

The Clown Bank

SANDRA'S GRANDMOTHER had given it to her a couple of years ago. Made of baked clay, the colorful clown bank stood eight inches high and maybe six inches wide. The artist had painted large red cheeks and blue eyes on his face and topped him off with a floppy green hat.

It was hard to see the coin slot across the top of the hat. Every week Sandra had slipped two or three quarters inside until the cheerful figure had become quite heavy.

Sandra held the clown upside down and pushed the blade of a kitchen knife in and out of the slot. With each thrust a quarter or two would escape from the bank. Impatiently she rattled the bank and begged it to release the coins faster.

"Come on, come on," Sandra coaxed the clown. "I've got to get going if I'm going to buy that tape."

Sandra had gone to a concert on the weekend but hadn't had enough cash to buy the group's tape. Angie had agreed to walk with her to the shopping mall today to pick up a copy.

"Six quarters!" Sandra growled at the clown as she shook it vigorously. "I need eleven bucks. Move it."

The clown never changed expressions, but Sandra's face grew more tense as she rapidly worked the knife in and out.

Two more quarters dropped from the bank and danced across the table top.

"A couple of bucks won't do it, ceramic brain. Angie's going to be ready." She put the knife down and shook the clown with greater force. The bank made a great deal of noise but not one coin appeared.

"You dumb clown!" Sandra threw her bank onto the carpeted floor. The clown bounced once and smashed against a chair leg. It broke open instantly, dumping quarters into a pile. Two coins rolled a few inches away and fell flat on their backs.

"No, no!" she screamed immediately. "Not my grandmother's clown."

Sandra sank to her knees and held her head in her hands.

☐

Be completely humble and gentle; be patient.

EPH. 4:2

☐

Questions for Family Discussion

Have you ever broken something because you were in too much of a hurry?

When you are upset, what do you do to calm down?

27

Cats and Cars

ARLY ONE EVENING Andy arranged a dozen of his miniature cars on the living room floor and sat down to play. Soon he lined a few cars up for a pretend race. Andy put a small white box to one side as a garage and then placed a black truck and a red '57 Chevy in it for repairs.

Within a few minutes, Claudia, the cat, very slowly and quietly tiptoed over to check out the territory. The cat rubbed against Andy's leg. She looked over the colorful cars. She purred.

Without warning, Claudia reached out and pushed a yellow racer with her paw.

"You leave my cars alone," Andy said firmly to his friend as he tapped her on the head.

Claudia had barely drawn back before her paw sprang out again. This time she sent three cars racing across the carpet.

"Butt out." Andy gave Claudia a good shove. "You keep that up and you're dog meat."

Standing erect, Claudia purred again. She sounded like she was thinking it over. Suddenly she marched in front of Andy, knocking the garage over and sending cars rolling.

"Fur-ball!" Andy shouted. He smacked the cat as she hurried away. "That's enough. You get near here again and you're going outside."

Claudia stood at the far side of the room and gazed at Andy. Her eyes darted from Andy to the cars, from the cars back to Andy. She then walked directly toward the cars. Without a "meow" she stepped over them all and sat down squarely on top of the small garage.

Andy screamed and pushed Claudia off the white box. The cat darted onto the couch. Andy grabbed the truck and heaved it at Claudia, but he hit the candy dish on the end table. The dish made a terrible noise as it crashed. Pieces of china flew in every direction.

☐

Anger is cruel and fury overwhelming.
PROV. 27:4

☐

Questions for Family Discussion

What kind of things make you mad?

Do you stay mad or do you get over it quickly?

Meet the Calderwoods

28

Tricky Teresa

LISA'S FINGERS were covered with paint so she wiped them on her blue smock. One more smear of paint was hardly noticeable among the hundreds already dotting the apron. She then added more white to the beautiful mane on her reddish-brown stallion. Cautiously, she tried to decide if it was too late to place a white spot on the horse's right front leg.

"Not a bad looking horse," Teresa said from Lisa's side.

"I don't know. His head looks crooked." Lisa wrinkled up her nose.

"It's a lot better than my goofy goat," Teresa droned. "I'm going to ask Mrs. Blackwell if it's too late to start over."

"Probably is." Lisa dabbed a white blotch on the horse's front leg. "There, I've done it. That doesn't look so bad, does it?"

"Well . . ."

"By the way, did you bring me the doll house furniture?" Lisa asked.

"Better yet, I brought the doll dresses. You're going to like those."

"I don't want the dresses. The deal was I get the furniture for a make-up lamp. You promised."

"Come on, I didn't exactly promise," Teresa objected.

"Of course you did. You said so yourself." Lisa grew red in the face.

"That's no big deal." Teresa motioned with her hands for Lisa to calm down. "Did you see my hands when we talked about the trade?"

"No. What was in your hands?"

"There wasn't anything in them; that's just the point. My right hand was at my side and my fingers were crossed."

"Hey, look, you crook." Lisa shook her paint brush at Teresa's nose. "I gave you my make-up light."

"Sure you did; but when you make a deal, always look to see if the other person's fingers are crossed. Crossed fingers mean you don't have to keep a promise. Everybody knows that."

"That's just an excuse for lying." Lisa's voice rose.

"It isn't either."

"How would you like it if . . ."

"Is there some problem here?" Mrs. Blackwell had joined them.

"This cheater is trying to. . . ."

"All right," Teresa cut off Lisa in mid-sentence. "I'll give you the lousy furniture. But I don't have to." She then shrugged her shoulders and returned to her desk.

☐

A scoundrel and villain,
who goes about with a corrupt mouth,
who winks with his eye,

signals with his feet
and motions with his fingers,
who plots evil with deceit in his heart—
he always stirs up dissension.

PROV. 6:12–14

☐

Questions for Family Discussion

Are you good at keeping your promises?

Have you ever used a trick to try to get out of a promise?

29

Shaking Fingers

*T*HIS SHOULDN'T *be hard,* Sandra thought as she walked into the store.

Look calm, she told herself. *They can't guess what I'm thinking. Be careful not to turn red. The clerk will think I'm just an average shopper. I am an average shopper. Well, almost.*

The earrings were mounted one pair to a card. Each card hung from a display rack. Sandra stopped and slowly turned the rack, her eyes looking for the clerk.

If Jenny can do this, so can I, she reasoned with herself. *I'll just take one set and slide it into my pocket. Then I'll walk directly toward the door as I planned. Stay calm,* she told herself.

Sandra looked at the silver earrings shaped like strawberries. She moved the rack and touched a red plastic pair.

They can't hear that, her mind said. *No one can hear my heart pounding. Get hold of yourself. This is crazy. As long as I don't turn red, I'll be all right.*

Stopping the rack, Sandra pulled off a card. The earrings were gold.

Why is my hand trembling? she asked herself under her breath. *Anyone can see me shaking. Go ahead,* she commanded herself, *put it in your pocket and get out of here. Do it. Do it.*

"May I help you?"

The clerk's voice startled Sandra. She dropped the earrings on the floor.

"No, no," Sandra's voice quivered. She stooped to pick up the earring card, but only dropped it again.

"That is, yes. Yes, you can. Where is the skirt department?"

"Why skirts are four aisles down and to your left," answered the bewildered lady.

"Exactly what I need," Sandra stuttered. "Can't have too many shirts, I mean skirts. Here, you keep these," she handed the card to the clerk.

"A blue skirt. That's what I need." Sandra hurried away. "Maybe a red one. It's so hard to decide."

She bumped into the next counter.

□

You shall not steal.

EX. 20:15

□

Questions for Family Discussion

How do people feel when we take their things?

Why do you think God commanded us not to steal?

30

Sick in Bed

D IDN'T YOU HEAR me call you?" Mrs. Calderwood said impatiently. "Why, you aren't even out of bed."

"I don't feel good," Mark answered, barely moving his lips. Claudia, the cat, sat on the pillow next to the boy's head. She sniffed at Mark's hair.

Mrs. Calderwood put her wrist on Mark's forehead, checking for a fever.

"I'm sick."

"You don't feel warm. Is it your stomach?"

"Kind of."

Claudia reached out to play with a shock of Mark's hair. The boy slowly pushed her paw away.

"You don't look pale, son." Mrs. Calderwood continued. "If you're sick, there must be some way you are sick."

"Maybe I have the mumps or Asian flu or malaria. How am I supposed to know what I have?"

"Let's call the doctor. We can probably get in this afternoon. You can explain to him how you caught a tropical disease."

"I don't need a doctor," Mark objected. "It's probably the twenty-four hour malaria."

Playfully, Claudia brushed Mark's hair. Mark pushed her off the bed.

"I know what your disease is. It's called book-reportitis. You didn't finish your report last night."

Mark paused, and then said quietly, "And Mrs. Pringle expects me to give the report to the class."

"You're afraid."

"Am not."

"Sure you are," his mother persisted. "You are afraid to go to school and just admit you messed up."

"I'm *not* afraid."

"It's all right to mess up. But when you do, you go to school and face the facts. You can't hide under the covers."

Claudia jumped up on the bed.

"Well, Dr. Mom has pronounced you cured and well. Get up and don't be late for school." Mrs. Calderwood turned and hurried out of the room.

"No one cares if I live or die around here," Mark barked.

Cautiously Claudia tiptoed over to Mark's head. Without warning she lay down on the boy's face.

"A-a-a-a-h! A-a-a-a-h! A-a-a-a-h!" The family could hear Mark from every part of the house.

☐

Do not let your hearts be troubled and do not be afraid.

JOHN 14:27

☐

Meet the Calderwoods

Questions for Family Discussion

Why is Mark afraid?

Have you ever been afraid because you did something wrong—or didn't do something you were expected to do?

Does it make you feel better to know Jesus is with you all the time?

31

Abraham, Isaac, and Jane Cup

MR. CALDERWOOD KNELT by the bed
with Andy close to his side. The second-grader placed
Nendo, the plastic space man, on the floor. He closed
his eyes and folded his hands.

"Can I pray first?" Andy asked.

"Sure."

"May the Father of Abraham, Isaac, and Jane Cup
watch over us . . ."

Mr. Calderwood tried to hold his giggle back but it
escaped. Andy stopped praying and looked up.

"I'm sorry I laughed," Mr. Calderwood said
sincerely. "It's just that I've never heard of Jane Cup."

"Sure you have. Mr. Toleffson always prays that in
church. Abraham, Isaac, and Jane Cup."

"No, that's Abraham, Isaac, and Jacob."

"Well, I can't remember all those names." Andy
folded his arms as his face dropped.

"You don't have to use all those names," Mr.
Calderwood explained lovingly. "That's Mr. Toleffson's
way of praying. You can pray any way you want to."

"I don't want to. It's too hard."

"You don't have any trouble talking to me. Prayer

102   **Meet the Calderwoods**

is just talking to God. He doesn't ask me to use other people's words," Mr. Calderwood continued. "Let's try it again and act like you are talking to me."

"What do I say?"

"Say what you feel. Is there something you want to thank God for? Is there something you need and would like to ask for? What about your friends? Would you like God to help Tony or Pat? Why not ask God to take care of your grandparents?"

"Just talk, like I'm talking to you?"

"Absolutely. We'll let Mr. Toleffson pray for Jane Cup."

☐

I always pray with joy.

PHIL. 1:4

☐

Questions for Family Discussion

What are some of the reasons that you can pray joyfully?

What relationships and things are you glad that God has given you? What would you like God to provide for you and your family? Perhaps you can include these in your prayers tonight.

32

The Farmyard

IT WAS EXACTLY the kind of work Lisa loved to do. She had collected different types of sticks and built a farmyard for history class. On the outside Lisa had erected a fence surrounding a pig pen, a horse corral, and a small log cabin. Building the cabin had been especially hard. She had broken each stick to the same size and laid them carefully one on the other.

Lisa completed the yard with some plastic animals from toy sets at home. She was extremely happy because the finished farmyard looked a lot like the drawing she had seen in her history book.

At least she was happy until Friday. When Lisa arrived at school that morning, she saw a large white soccer ball sitting in the middle of her project. Part of the fence was torn down. The pig pen was wrecked. And her cabin was totally smashed.

Lisa picked up the soccer ball, mumbled a few words to herself, and fought hard not to cry. She could feel a large lump in her throat.

When Lisa had free time during the day, she worked at putting the yard back together. Mrs. Norman said she would wait until next week to grade it.

THE FARMYARD **105**

Even though Lisa stayed thirty minutes after school, the farmyard was still unfinished. The cabin was tricky, so it would have to wait until Monday. But Lisa could handle it; she could handle most things well. She put on her best smile and headed down the hall.

By the water fountain she saw Ted just hanging around.

"I'm sorry," he said.

"Yeah, thanks," Lisa replied. "But I'll put it back together."

"No, I mean I'm sorry I did it."

"You did it?" Lisa couldn't believe her ears. "That's all right. Accidents happen."

"But it wasn't an accident," Ted continued. "I did it on purpose."

"You rat! You mean you dumped that ball on my project?"

"I said I was sorry."

"I'll sorry you. Wait till Mrs. Norman hears about this. What if somebody wrecked your project?" Lisa insisted.

"I don't blame you for being angry. But I thought I should tell you that I did it. And I'm sorry."

Lisa paused a minute and thought about how much she liked Ted and how much fun they always had together. "Ah, so what?" she said. "You can't stay mad at friends. Did I ever tell you what I did to my neighbor's tulips? You can't tell anyone about this. Promise?"

Lisa and Ted walked toward the exit doors talking and laughing.

□

Then Peter came to Jesus and asked, "Lord, how many times shall I forgive my

Meet the Calderwoods

brother when he sins against me? Up to seven times?"

Jesus answered, "I tell you, not seven times, but seventy-seven times."

MATT. 18:21–22

□

Questions for Family Discussion

Is there someone you have trouble forgiving? Would you feel better if you could forgive him?

Do you believe that God has forgiven you?

Assignment: Read pages 49-55 in Our World

The Missing Sweater

THE CALDERWOOD FAMILY had just finished eating when Sandra made her announcement.

"Would everyone please remain seated?" she insisted. "There is one matter I would like to clear up."

"Do we have to put up with this?" Lisa, Sandra's younger sister, demanded.

"I'm sure this doesn't involve me." Andy began to rise from his chair.

"Not too quickly," his father interrupted. "Let's see what Sandra wants."

Mrs. Calderwood agreed.

"Thank you," Sandra continued. "This should not take long. Andy, let me see your fingertips."

Andy cooperated.

"You are in the clear. And now for Lisa's fingertips."

"This is silly," Lisa objected.

"It will only take a second," Mr. Calderwood added.

"All right. Here." Lisa pushed her hands forward and gave everyone a quick glimpse. She then shoved her hands rapidly under the table.

"You move fast," said Sandra. "But I could see what looks like dirt around your nails. You are guilty of going into my closet and taking my clothes without asking."

"How do you know that?" asked Andy.

"This morning I put black shoe polish on the bottom side of my closet doorknob. I knew the thief couldn't get all the polish off his hands."

"All I did was borrow a sweater," Lisa insisted. "You make it sound like I'm a criminal."

"I'm afraid Sandra does have a point," Mrs. Calderwood concluded. "No one likes to have his personal things taken without being asked."

"Okay, book me," Lisa mocked. "Give me bread and water; send me to the chair. I'm the sweater thief."

"You aren't a thief. You're a borrower. But it helps a lot if we ask before we borrow. Everyone feels better that way," Mrs. Calderwood said.

☐

> *Give to the one who asks you, and do not turn away from the one who wants to borrow from you.*
>
> MATT. 5:42

☐

THE MISSING SWEATER **109**

Questions for Family Discussion

Has someone ever taken something from you without asking? How did it make you feel?

Are you generous by loaning your things to your brothers and sisters?

Andy Just Stared

H AS ANYONE seen my books?" Sandra walked out of the kitchen to search.

Mark reached for the syrup and began to flood his pancakes.

Lisa read the back of the cereal box but was too tired to talk.

And Andy just stared.

"Stack the dishes in the dishwasher," Mrs. Calderwood reminded them. "I'll wash them after work."

"H'm" is all Mr. Calderwood said as he read the newspaper.

And Andy just stared.

"What's wrong with the spaceman?" Mark pointed to Andy.

"Couldn't sleep last night," Lisa said, barely moving her lips. "He got up and watched the late show."

"Oh my, what movie was it?" Mrs. Calderwood asked.

"I think it was *The Mummy Eats Michigan*. Pretty gory stuff," Lisa explained.

"He knows better than to watch monster movies.

They always upset him." Mrs. Calderwood stood up and rubbed the back of Andy's neck.

And Andy just stared.

"Someone took my books," Sandra ranted as she walked back through the kitchen.

"Why didn't you tell me you couldn't sleep?" Mrs. Calderwood asked Andy. "You've got to snap awake." She pushed a spoonful of cereal to his lips.

"Let's think good thoughts. Wash those monsters right out of your brain," she added cheerfully.

"Think of something beautiful like me," Lisa suggested.

"School is calling you back from the land of the dead," Mrs. Calderwood said as she helped Andy up from his chair and led him toward the bathroom.

As she put toothpaste on his brush, Mrs. Calderwood added, "Next time, couldn't you watch a musical?"

And Andy just stared.

☐

Finally, brothers, whatever is true, whatever is noble, whatever is right, whatever is pure, whatever is lovely, whatever is admirable—if anything is excellent or praiseworthy—think about such things.

PHIL. 4:8

☐

Meet the Calderwoods

Questions for Family Discussion

Have you ever watched a movie that you knew would give you nightmares? Which one?

Have you ever turned off a movie because you knew it would bother you?

Have you ever turned off a movie because you knew it would bother someone in the room?

35

Poor Pluto

BET YOU CAN'T name all nine of them."
Lisa jumped on the couch and scooted close to her
mother.

"Give me a clue; all nine of what?" Mrs. Calderwood put the newspaper on her lap.

"You know, the planets."

"Oh, the nine planets. Well, let's start at the beginning."

"Mom, I don't want a long speech, just the nine
planets."

"Don't rush me. What is a planet?"

"You know, one of those big jobbies that runs
around the sun," Lisa sounded exasperated.

"Got ya. One of those large bodies that revolves
around the sun. That must be Mars, Venus, Mercury,
Neptune. Now that's four."

"Good start; you have five to go."

"There must be Saturn, Uranus, and the moon."

"No! The moon doesn't run around the sun. It
runs around the Earth."

"I knew that. I was just testing you." Mrs. Calderwood winked. "How about Earth?"

"Got it. That's seven."

"Maybe Jupiter."

"Got it. One more."

"Oh, that pesky little thing called Pluto."

"Yeah! You did it."

"Only thing is, Pluto may stop being a planet."

"How can you stop being a planet?" Lisa's upper lip twisted. "Can you be a planet one day and a star the next?"

"Not exactly. But what I read was that Pluto is so small and so far away that astronomers may have made a mistake in calling it a planet. Some moons may be larger than Pluto."

"You can't count on anything. I finally memorized the planets and one of them turns out to be just a fat rock."

"That's not all. Sometimes Pluto is the planet farthest from the sun and sometimes Neptune is farthest."

"It's crazy."

"Not really. So far it's held together pretty well."

"Yea, at least we know the moon isn't really made of cheese."

"That isn't all. The important thing is that our heavenly Father, who created the planets, never changes. God is steady day in and day out."

"Even if Pluto falls into the sea." Lisa bounded off the couch.

□

Every good and perfect gift is from above, coming down from the Father of the heavenly lights, who does not change like shifting shadows.

JAMES 1:17

POOR PLUTO   **115**

Questions for Family Discussion

What did God create that you think is particularly neat?

What good gifts has God given you?

36

How the Ball Bounces

SANDRA LEAPT UP in the air smoothly to make the jump shot. The basketball bounced off the backboard and she hurried for the rebound. Instead of taking a second shot, however, Sandra tossed the ball to her friend Beth.

The two girls had stayed after practice to sharpen up for the intramural game on Thursday. Beth threw the ball at the net but it fell short. Sandra grabbed the ball on the first bounce and dribbled over to her friend.

"Not much zip today, huh?"

"I guess not." Beth's eyes filled with water but the tears seemed locked in.

"Is the divorce still tearing you up?" Sandra hugged the ball.

"I feel like a dope. You would think I could pull it together by now. My parents have been divorced for nearly four months."

"That's got to be a bummer."

"You know the worst part?" Beth folded her arms and looked at the floor. "Nobody wants to hear about it."

"I felt that way, too." Sandra held the ball against

HOW THE BALL BOUNCES

117

her stomach. "You remember at the beginning of the year when Mrs. Kramer and I were going at it in English? I couldn't find any way to make her happy."

"It did look like she had it in for you." Beth shifted her weight to one leg.

"Anyway I interpreted a story, she always said I was wrong," said Sandra.

"So how did you handle it?" Beth took the ball from Sandra.

"I talked to Bunson, the school counselor."

"And he chewed her out or what?" Beth put a spin on the ball as she dribbled.

"Oh no, that's not the way Bunson operates. He told me how to handle people when they are difficult. He showed me how to relax and back off. She still ticks me off but not like she used to."

"Sometimes I really need someone to talk to." As Beth dribbled the ball, a boy walking by stuck out his foot and kicked the ball across the gym.

"Yeah, especially with so many dips running around," Sandra laughed.

☐

Listen to advice and accept instruction,
and in the end you will be wise.
PROV. 19:20

☐

Questions for Family Discussion

If you had a problem, who would you talk to about it?

Have you ever asked someone for advice and received some good help?

HOW THE BALL BOUNCES

37

Smoke Rings

Y OU THOUGHT you were pretty smart, smoking in the locker room," Mr. Janzen, the assistant principal, said with a gruff voice and a stern look.

"I wasn't smoking," Mark replied shakily.

"There is no sense lying, Mark. Coach Trepton caught both you and Derrick."

"But I wasn't smoking."

"Derrick has been suspended for one day and his mother has to come to school," Mr. Janzen continued. He rapped a pencil on his desk without moving his eyes from Mark. "You might as well tell the truth."

"I am, Mr. Janzen. Honest. Derrick and I were sitting on the bench when he lit up a cigarette. He asked if I could blow smoke rings and I said no."

"And you are trying to tell me he was the only one smoking?"

"There wasn't anything I could do. What was I supposed to do, get up and leave?"

"Nobody was keeping you there. I need to call your parents and ask them to come to school." Mr. Janzen's hand reached for the telephone.

"Please don't." Mark leaned forward. "I don't know how I can prove I wasn't smoking."

"In my experience, if one boy is smoking the other guy almost always has a cigarette, too." He picked up the receiver and looked down at a note with the Calderwood phone number on it.

"What did Coach say?" Mark spoke rapidly. "He didn't really see me smoking, did he?"

"And I'm supposed to believe you were sitting there watching Derrick smoke? You must think I was born yesterday."

"I don't know why I was sitting there. He said he would show me smoke rings; that's all I know."

"What if he wanted to show you how to rob lockers or he said 'Watch while I set the uniforms on fire'? I suppose you would have sat still through that, too." Mr. Janzen looked up through his glasses.

"No, of course not, but that's different."

"Not much," the assistant principal barked back. "Mark, you're lucky. Coach Trepton didn't see you smoking and I pretty much believe your story. But you better be careful who you pick for friends. Sometimes when a net is thrown out, everybody gets caught in it.

"Now, get out of here."

☐

A righteous man is cautious in friendship.
PROV. 12:26

☐

Questions for Family Discussion

What did Mark do wrong in this story?

Sometimes our friends do bad things. How can we decide when it's best that we try to help our friends, and when should we decide that it's time to stop hanging around them?

The Embarrassing Penknife

I HAVE NEVER been so embarrassed in all my life." Sandra threw her Bible on the end table as she hurried into the living room.

"What happened now?" Mr. Calderwood put down the magazine he had just picked up.

"I'll never show my face in that church again. I was totally humiliated." Sandra flopped onto the couch.

"This is starting to sound serious. Calm down and tell us what happened," her father urged.

"Don't ask me what happened. I'm not the one who did it. I must have turned red in front of everybody."

"Maybe when you get hold of yourself you can explain what is behind all of this."

"Ask Andy. Don't drill me. Just ask the young Mr. Calderwood. The *very* young *immature* Mr. Calderwood."

Andy squirmed on the floor but didn't volunteer any information. Sandra lurched to her feet.

"Don't leave," Mr. Calderwood directed Sandra. "Now I'm curious. What did Andy do?"

"When they took the offering this morning, after

you passed on the plate, your bright young son put in his penknife. Just dumped it right in and passed it on."

"That sounds different," her father conceded.

"Oh! And everybody along the pew saw the penknife as it passed down the row. I thought Mrs. Trautman was going to have a stroke. And naturally Doyle had a giggling fit. I'm switching churches next Sunday. That's it."

"Andy," said Mr. Calderwood. "Did you really put your penknife in the offering plate?"

"I suppose." Andy didn't look up.

"You don't see that every Sunday. Would you like to tell Sandra why you did that?"

"No."

"Well, I think it would be helpful. I'm sure you had a great reason; you don't give penknives away. Why don't you explain it to me then?"

"There's nothing wrong with it," Andy insisted.

"'Nothing wrong' he says. I'll never be able to face my friends again." Sandra's voice remained high-pitched.

"I believe you had a good reason, son. Help me understand it," Mr. Calderwood asked gently.

"They said Allen was real sick so I prayed for him and he got better."

"He did, Andy. That's true. And the penknife?" Mr. Calderwood continued.

"I gave that to God as a present for helping Allen," Andy answered firmly.

"That proves it. Andy is the one who needs help." Sandra hurried out of the room.

"I don't think so." Mr. Calderwood picked up his magazine. "I don't think so."

□

I will sacrifice a thank offering to you
and call on the name of the Lord.

PS. 116:17

□

Questions for Family Discussion

For what are you thankful to God?

What are some of the ways you can give God a "thank offering"?

39

Stuttering Sam

'M. HI, Sam," a boy said mockingly as he walked by the lunch table. His four friends burst out laughing as they continued toward the cafeteria line.

Sam blushed as he sat alone eating his lunch. His weak attempt to smile back only showed how hurt he felt.

As the boys entered the cafeteria line, they found Lisa Calderwood selecting her food.

"Hey," Matt blurted out to Lisa. "Did you meet the new kid, old Stuttering Sam? Man, is he a riot."

"Yeah, it takes him five minutes just to say 'good morning,'" added Lennie.

They all laughed again.

"Sometime ask him what time it is, if you have an hour to spare," Kevin chimed in.

Lisa didn't say anything, but the boys noticed that she didn't join in the laughter. She finished choosing her food, handed in her lunch ticket, and began looking for a table. Almost like a magnet her eyes were drawn to a boy in a red striped shirt who was sitting all alone.

"May I sit with you?" Without waiting for an answer Lisa wiggled onto the bench beside him.

126   **Meet the Calderwoods**

"S . . . s . . . sure. My name is S . . . S . . . Sam."

"Are you new or something?"

"We just moved here from Seattle. A . . . a . . . and I'm learning my way around."

"You are going to . . . ." Lisa was interrupted by two girls.

"Hey, wel . . . wel . . . wel . . . come to sch . . . sch . . . school," one of the girls teased Sam, and then the pair hustled off giggling.

"Don't pay them any mind. They make fun of everybody." Lisa stuck a straw in her chocolate milk.

"I kn . . . kn . . . know it sounds funny when I stutt . . . stutter."

"Forget it. It doesn't sound near as strange as some of the awful words some of those guys use."

"I hadn't thought of th . . . th . . . that."

"If we ignore them, making fun of people will get old. I bet they'll soon lay off."

"I'm seeing a ther . . . a . . . therapist. My mom says she c . . . c . . . can see a difference already."

"Hang in there." Lisa slurped her milk. "Why don't you and I eat lunch together for a week or two? There's no need for you to sit here alone.

"By the way," Lisa added, "have you met Mrs. Magler yet? Boy, is she strict."

☐

The King will reply, "I tell you the truth, whatever you did for one of the least of these brothers of mine, you did for me."
MATT. 25:40

Questions for Family Discussion

Do you know someone who gets picked on a lot?

Is there some way you could help make his life a little easier?

40

Daddy-daughter Date Night

N UMBER SIX!"
Immediately two people exploded toward the center of the room and stopped where the red bandanna was laying on the floor. The eleven-year-old girl bounced around on the arches of her feet trying to trick her opponent. Opposite her, her father, with arms outstretched, moved carefully, hoping to prevent the girl from scooping up the bandanna.

"He moves pretty good for a dad," Sandra told Vickie amid the noise.

"I guess, but look at those old buzzards," Vickie laughed.

"You're telling me," Sandra agreed.

A tremendous cheer went up as the girl snatched the bandanna and darted safely back to the circle of spectators.

"Those dads are starting to lose their hair," Vickie giggled.

"That's nothing. Most of the dads have potbellies. You think our husbands will look like that?" Sandra wondered.

"ELEVEN!" the leader sang out.

Another girl and another father hurried toward the center and began prancing around the flag.

"I'll tell you one thing, my husband isn't taking those Sunday afternoon naps. You'd think my dad was a hundred years old or something," Vickie added.

"And my husband isn't listening to that corny music," Sandra said. "Can you believe what my parents listen to? It'll drive you crazy."

"SIXTEEN!"

Like broncos two more contestants broke for the red cloth.

"At least your dad doesn't tell those awful jokes like my dad does." Vickie shook her head.

"Are you kidding?" Sandra objected. "He about embarrasses me to death. You never know what he's going to say."

"But my dad's still a pretty good guy," Vickie conceded.

"Oh, mine too."

"When it comes down to it, my dad would do anything for me." Vickie smiled.

"Like take you to a Daddy-daughter Date Night," Sandra laughed.

"Yeah, he's not a bad guy for being so decrepit," Vickie agreed.

"TWELVE!"

Sandra bolted for the center.

□

"Honor your father and mother"—which is the first commandment with a promise—"that it may go well with you and that you may enjoy long life on the earth."
EPH. 6:2–3

Meet the Calderwoods

Questions for Family Discussion

What do you like about your parents?

What do you enjoy doing with your parents?

Do you ever thank God for your parents?

41

The Red Sock and the Green Sock

Y OU CAN'T GO to church like *that*," Sandra growled.

"Like what?" asked Andy.

"Look at your socks. A red one and a green one. People will laugh at you," she explained.

"I think they look pretty good."

"Andy." Mr. Calderwood's voice stopped the boy in his tracks. "Two red socks look good. Two green socks look good. What you have on looks dumb."

As Andy disappeared upstairs, the family could hear him mumbling to himself. A few minutes later he strolled slowly back into the living room.

"Now that's better," said Mr. Calderwood without bothering to look. "What?" he gasped as his eyes finally found his son's socks. "No, no, that won't do. A gray sock and a brown sock!"

Andy's shoulders drooped as he started toward his room. "I don't have two socks that match."

"Wait a minute." Mr. Calderwood looked confused. "Are you serious? How can a seven-year-old boy not have two socks that match?"

"It's not my fault." Andy sounded sincere. "I leave

my socks on the floor and Clyde always takes one. Then I can never find it."

"Explain that again," Mr. Calderwood said impatiently. "You leave your socks on the floor and the dog steals one?"

"And it's not my fault."

"Anybody too lazy to pick up his socks deserves to lose them." Mr. Calderwood roared with laughter. "Maybe you had better wear a gray one and a brown one to church and be Two-Toned Andy."

And he laughed some more.

□

If a man is lazy, the rafters sag;
if his hands are idle, the house leaks.
                                ECCL. 10:18

□

Questions for Family Discussion

Are you good at picking things up?

How would you describe your bedroom?

Can you think of something you lost or broke because you failed to put it away?

42

School Stinks

THE MINUTE she collapsed at her desk, Michelle declared, "School stinks."

"Good morning," Sandra said, trying to be upbeat.

"You know how Mr. Langston will start the class: 'Now, let's pay attention, boys and girls.' Doesn't that scrape your bones?"

"I suppose, but you get used to it."

"Not really." Michelle shuffled her books. "If the principal could see how he runs this class, Mr. Langston would disappear from here quicker than a bad dream."

"You're off to a great start." Sandra took out her homework and put it on the corner of her desk.

"Hey, it's not me. It's this lousy school. My cousin from Spokane can't believe the stories I tell her about this jail. She says if she went here her parents would march right in and really make a fuss."

"Sure it isn't perfect, but. . . ."

"Perfect? 'Isn't perfect' she says. It's a blotch on the name of education, if you ask me."

"S-h-h-h," Sandra moved her eyebrows to indicate that Mr. Langston had entered the room.

"Great gobs, look at that shirt. Somewhere there is a blimp running around naked."

That caught Sandra by surprise and she barely muffled a laugh. Meanwhile, Mr. Langston started to write instructions on the chalk board.

"He prints in block letters like we're in the second grade," Michelle said contemptuously.

"Don't you ever say anything nice?" Sandra wondered.

"When there is something nice to say, you can count on me. But you can't call a pig a tiger. This school is the pits. Everybody knows that."

"Come on," Sandra begged. "Tell me one good thing about school. You can do it."

" 'One good thing,' she asks. All right, we don't go to school on Saturdays."

"Man, you're grouchy today," Sandra declared.

" 'Grouchy,' she calls me. 'Grouchy.' I'd be in a great mood if it wasn't for school. This place would depress Mr. Rogers' Neighborhood."

"There are a lot of things I really enjoy about school. It doesn't get me down," said Sandra.

"Be careful, Sandra. When you like school, that's the first sign you're going brain dead."

"I'm not going to let it turn me into a grouch."

"There she goes again, calling me a grouch. I tell you, it's this school."

Mr. Langston turned, faced the class and said, "Now, let's pay attention, boys and girls."

☐

Finally, brothers, whatever is true, whatever is noble, whatever is right, whatever is pure, whatever is lovely, whatever is admi-

rable—if anything is excellent or praisewor-
thy—think about such things.

☐

Questions for Family Discussion

What do you *really* like about school?

Have you *ever* tried to think about the good things at home, church, or school? Does that help?

43

Collecting Cars

WHILE THE ADULTS drank coffee in the living room, Andy and his friend Bouton faded away to Andy's bedroom. Bouton, born in an Asian refugee camp, had arrived in the United States only three months before. Fortunately, he had learned a great deal of English before coming.

"Want to see my car collection?" Without waiting for an answer, Andy pulled at the top drawer. The drawer jammed.

"I've been collecting them a long time," Andy continued. "I've got so many now I can't even get to them half the time. That's why I keep this kitchen knife on the dresser."

Andy slid the blade into the dresser drawer and began pressing down the boxes of cars. It was no easy task, because three or four boxes were so high that they prevented the drawer from opening.

"Have you started your car collection yet?"

"No, not yet." Bouton grinned.

"It must be hard at first. But when your dad gets a regular job, you can get some cars. Plus my grandmother gives me cars for my birthday and Christmas. Oh yeah, you don't have a grandmother. She died in the camp, right?"

Andy didn't look up as he worked intently on releasing the drawer.

"That's a tough break. Losing your grandmother and all. Maybe you could get a paper route and make money. Then you could buy your cars.

"There, I've got it."

The open drawer revealed dozens of cars. Racing cars, trucks, motorcycles, a couple of airplanes, a helicopter, two spaceships. Many of the toys were still in the original boxes.

"They look good." Bouton smiled as Andy handed him a black sports car with a silver dual exhaust.

"I'm going to have to use a second drawer if I'm going to keep collecting these." Andy picked up a couple more boxes. "You can't have too many cars."

Andy looked at Bouton's happy face and suddenly stopped talking. The wheels were turning in his brain.

"Maybe I'm wrong. Maybe you can get too many cars. You keep that one."

"Oh, I couldn't do that," Bouton protested.

"Sure you can. And this one, too. And what about this Trans Am?" Andy piled cars onto his friend's hands. "I want to start your car collection. Besides you would do me a big favor. Now I'll be able to get my drawer closed."

☐

Good will come to him who is generous.

PS. 112:5

☐

Questions for Family Discussion

How would you describe your attitude toward sharing?

Have you ever given something away that you really liked?

Do you enjoy being generous or stingy?

Meet the Calderwoods

44

Collapsing on the Couch

O H, DAD," Lisa gasped as she walked to the couch and threw herself down. "Feel my forehead. I'm dying. Call the minister. Plan my funeral."

Mr. Calderwood looked over the newspaper he was reading. "H'm," he said slowly.

"You don't understand. I'm totally exhausted. We played volleyball after school, then right after dinner I had to run over to Lori's house to finish English. I've put in a twelve-hour day. Look, my eyes are bloodshot."

"H'm."

"My heart is racing. I must be getting dizzy. It's too late for an ambulance. Just pull a blanket over me." Lisa lay motionless on the couch.

"Before you die," Mr. Calderwood said dryly, "tell me exactly what your problem is."

"You mean you can't tell? I'm overworked, abused, misunderstood; I'm on the borderline of a total breakdown."

"It sounds like you want something."

"It's probably too late." Lisa placed her hand over her heart. "But . . . but maybe if someone could do my dishes tonight, I just might pull through. I know that's

COLLAPSING ON THE COUCH **141**

asking a lot, but it's probably my only chance to survive."

"What in the world is all the noise in here?" Mrs. Calderwood said as she entered the room.

"You're just in time, honey. Lisa seems to be breathing her last."

"O-h-h-h-h!" Lisa groaned.

"She has decided that if someone doesn't do her dishes, the work will kill her for sure," Mr. Calderwood explained.

"Oh, the dishes," Lisa's mother smiled. "I've already done those. I knew you would need a little help tonight. You might as well sit up and live." Mrs. Calderwood left the room.

"You can relax. It looks like death has decided to pass you by this time," said her dad.

"I can't believe that." Lisa sat up. "I didn't even have to talk her into it."

□

Instead, be kind to each other, tenderhearted, forgiving one another, just as God has forgiven you because you belong to Christ.
EPH. 4:32 LB

□

Questions for Family Discussion

What are some ways you could help a parent when he or she doesn't feel well?

What are some ways you could help a brother or sister who doesn't feel well?

45

Prune Face

WHEN SANDRA FINALLY forced her locker open, books tumbled onto the hallway floor. She growled and bent over to pick them up when the bell rang. It was time for class to start and she was still shuffling through her things.

Sandra arrived late to class.

"Thank you for attending class today, Miss Calderwood," Mr. Lanier said from the front of the classroom. "When you find it convenient, please put everything away except your social studies book."

Sandra grumbled under her breath as she stacked her books and sorted out her papers. The pile of books began to slide.

BANG! Her math book hit the floor.

"Sorry, Mr. Lanier." She grimaced and picked up the runaway volume.

"Would you care to go out and come in again, maybe when you are better organized?"

"Nope! Nope! I can handle it," she protested.

Randy leaned over from the next desk and whispered, "Boy, are you a prune face."

Sandra stuck out her tongue.

"Your face is shriveled up like a prune."

"Shush!" she said loud enough for the teacher to hear.

Mr. Lanier turned slowly from the chalkboard and stared at the flustered fifth grader.

"Mr. Lanier," Sandra said loudly and clearly, "I'll take you up on that invitation."

"*What* invitation?" he asked impatiently.

"The one to leave the room and come in again." She stood without waiting for his response and walked boldly out the door.

Within ten seconds the door opened and Sandra reappeared, complete with a broad smile. Moving directly to her seat she announced, "Let the class begin."

Sandra then turned to Randy, showed him her white teeth, and winked.

☐

A happy heart makes the face cheerful.
PROV. 15:13

☐

Questions for Family Discussion

Have you ever said to yourself that you felt grouchy and decided to change your attitude?

If you have a problem, can you sometimes forget that problem and go ahead and enjoy the day?

46

The Super Modern House

WHAT ARE you drawing?" Shawn stretched his neck to see Mark's desk.

"It's just a sketch."

"Of what?" Shawn curled his lip.

"Nothing really." Mark kept drawing.

"I can tell that. I thought it was a shipwreck."

"You're really funny," Mark replied irritably.

"No kidding," Shawn persisted. "What is that strange room on the side?"

"It's an observatory. The family will use it to check out stars."

"Nah, no home has an observatory. If you're rich you get a swimming pool, but no goofy observatory." Shawn slumped back into his seat and picked up his comic book.

"Well, this home will," Mark mumbled.

"Just don't let Mrs. Slifer catch you doing that in study hall."

"Me! What about your comic book!"

"That's different." Shawn leaned forward again. "Boys are supposed to read comic books; they aren't supposed to draw weird buildings. Now, what's that?"

THE SUPER MODERN HOUSE   **147**

"You wouldn't understand."

"Try me."

"It's a feeding box for deer," Mark added shyly.

"That's it. You're ready for the loony bin. Like Bambi is going to trot up to your backyard and munch on your mom's home cooking."

"Why don't you go back to your comic book and give your brain a rest." Mark slapped his sketch inside the desk.

"*My* brain a rest? You don't catch me drawing goofy houses and junk like that."

Mark picked up his sociology book and started turning the pages. A lump formed in his throat as he thought about the cruel things Shawn had said. None of the pages came into focus as Mark thumbed through the book aimlessly.

Suddenly Mark closed the book and slammed it on the desk. He abruptly pulled his sketch out and picked up his pen.

"Wait till you see what I'm going to put on it next," Mark whispered.

"H'm." Shawn didn't bother to look up.

☐

Reckless words pierce like a sword.
PROV. 12:18

☐

Questions for Family Discussion

How does it feel when someone makes fun of what you are doing?

Are you careful not to put down other people's plans?

How good are you at complimenting others?

47

Lunch Money

DO YOU WANT a chocolate cupcake or would you just throw it away?" Mrs. Calderwood held the cupcake and waited for Sandra's decision.

"Well," Sandra thought as she fixed a bologna and cheese sandwich. "I might as well take it. I can trade it off for chips or something."

"There are celery sticks in the fridge."

"I'll grab some of those." Sandra dropped her sandwich into a plastic bag.

"Money for a drink is on the counter. I've got to get ready for work," Mrs. Calderwood said as she started to leave the kitchen. "Oh, speaking of money: Did you ever pay back Kim?"

"For what?"

"You remember, the $1.50 you borrowed when you forgot your lunch."

"I'll remember. Don't you worry." Sandra picked up her lunch bag.

"Just a minute, young lady." Mrs. Calderwood stopped and faced Sandra. "You mean it's a week later and you still haven't paid back Kim?"

"I will, Mom; I just forget."

"What kind of friend is that? Take $1.50 off the counter and pay her today. You can't borrow something and forget to return it."

"Mom, I'm in no mood for this. I've got to get to school."

"Stand still, Miss Calderwood." Her mother opened a kitchen drawer.

"You aren't going to do anything dumb, are you?"

"Nothing dumb, but paying back your debts is terribly important."

"I took the money to school one day but I forgot to give it to Kim." Sandra's voice rose.

"Good intentions do not get the job done." Mrs. Calderwood took Sandra's right hand. "Hold your finger out."

"Mom!"

Mrs. Calderwood tied a red string around Sandra's ring finger.

"I can't believe this. You're treating me like a child."

"You're like everyone else. We forget to do what is right, so we need little reminders."

"I can't believe my own mother expects me to wear a red string around my finger."

"This way I bet you will pay back Kim during the first few minutes you are in school today." Mrs. Calderwood muffled her laugh as she left the kitchen.

□

*Keep my commands and you will live;
guard my teachings as the apple of your
eye.*

*Bind them on your fingers; write them on
the tablet of your heart.*
                              PROV. 7:2–3

□

Questions for Family Discussion

Are you good at paying back what you borrow?

How do you help yourself remember what God teaches us in the Bible?

Do you read the Bible, memorize verses, attend Sunday school classes?

48

Glue in the Lock

WHAT IN THE WORLD is wrong with this dumb thing?" Shawn smashed his lock against his hall locker. "My key won't fit. The stupid thing fit yesterday."

The commotion had drawn a small crowd of students on their way to the next class. Shawn's friend, Mike, gave the lock a close look.

"Cement," Mike announced. "Somebody put glue in the lock."

"What bonehead did this?" Shawn asked.

Coach Trepton was attracted to the racket.

"What's this all about?" he asked.

"Somebody put glue in Shawn's lock," Mike explained. "Now he can't get his key in it."

"Yeah, and all my books are in there," Shawn added.

"Tell the custodian. Mr. Larson might be able to pick the glue out," said Coach. "If not he will have to saw through the lock. The rest of you, get to class."

Students began to scurry down the hall.

"Oh, Calderwood," the coach called out.

"I'm late for English," Mark objected.

"I know you'd hate to miss a good English class, but you'd better come to my office this hour."

"Why me, Coach?" Mark said as they walked toward the gym.

"Because I happen to know that Shawn hid your books Wednesday, and I hear you were pretty ticked about it."

"That doesn't mean anything," Mark insisted.

"Let me see your hands."

Mark reluctantly lifted his right hand for the coach to inspect. He then shifted his books and displayed his left.

"That wouldn't be glue on your fingers, now would it?"

"Nobody said anything when he hid *my* books."

"Probably not. It's usually the person who tries to get even that gets in trouble. Just like in football; the guy who hits back usually gets the whistle," said Coach.

"That's not fair."

"No, it isn't fair, but it's a fact. People who try to retaliate often end up in the most trouble," the coach said as they entered the office. "Have a seat."

☐

When they hurled their insults at him, he did not retaliate; when he suffered, he made no threats. Instead, he entrusted himself to him who judges justly.
1 PETER 2:23

☐

Meet the Calderwoods

Questions for Family Discussion

Do you try to get even with those who hurt you? How have you tried?

Has someone ever hurt you or your feelings, and you decided not to get even? Did that make you feel good or bad? Why?

49

Spacemen

ANDY UNWRAPPED his new astronaut and put it in the briefcase next to the other three. They were surrounded by two spacecrafts, a space lab, and one cosmonaut.

"Want to see my collection?" Andy called to his father as Mr. Calderwood walked by.

"You bet." Mr. Calderwood paused. "Oh, great, that's my briefcase. I need that for work."

"It's my collection case," Andy objected as he fumbled with the keys to the case.

"Not really. You're using it for your collection but I really have to take it to work. Let's see if we can find you a box or something."

"I don't want a box. I need a case," Andy pouted.

"That's fine. Maybe you can get a case at the hobby store when you go to the mall. I think I know where there's a box you can use for now."

Andy dropped his bottom lip, tightened his forehead, and glared.

In a few minutes Mr. Calderwood returned. "This

Meet the Calderwoods

isn't real fancy but it will do for now." He placed a large cereal box next to Andy.

"Come on, Dad," Andy pleaded. "You can get a new briefcase when you go to the mall." Andy looped his arms around the open case.

"Don't be unreasonable, son."

"Here, take it." Andy threw the keys inside the case and slammed the lid shut.

"That isn't locked, is it?" Mr. Calderwood demanded.

"I don't know." Andy shrunk back.

Mr. Calderwood pulled vigorously but the lid stubbornly held tight.

"Of course it is. Of course it is. You have quite a temper, pal."

"It wasn't my fault." Andy looked at the floor.

"It certainly was your fault. Just because you didn't get your way, you threw a fit."

"Don't you have a second key?" Andy asked sheepishly.

"Sure I have an extra key. It's in the case with the other key."

☐

A quick-tempered man does foolish things.
PROV. 14:17

☐

Questions for Family Discussion

What would life be like if God had a quick, bad temper?

Do you ever throw a fit? What's that like?

What do you do to stop from throwing a fit? Count to ten?

50

A Gift of Strawberries

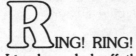ING! RING!

Lisa bounded off the couch and opened the door. Mrs. Towson was standing on the porch with a white box in her hands.

"Come in. Come in," Lisa insisted.

"Well, thank you."

"Nobody's home but me. What's in the box?" Lisa gently pulled at the cardboard container and peeked inside.

"Strawberries! Fantastic. Did these come out of your garden?" Lisa rattled on.

"Why, yes, they did. And I ... "

"You are so good at this. My mom said just last week that you are the best gardener in the county."

"Well, thank you. But I was wondering ..."

"Do you put real sugar on them when you serve them? My mom likes to use that phony sugar but I don't think they taste as good. What do you think?"

Lisa steadily pulled the box out of Mrs. Towson's hands.

"Four quarts!" Lisa exclaimed. "You are a generous lady to give away strawberries. What an attitude."

Lisa held the box in her arms.

"I'm not sure you understand," Mrs. Towson added hesitantly.

"I understand all right. You are one big-hearted person. I'll have my mom call you as soon as she gets home. You washed them and everything."

"You see, I was next door ... "

"I bet you gave them a box of strawberries, too. I'm not surprised. I'll put them in the refrigerator. That will keep them fresh."

"As I was trying to say, I was next door ... "

"How many quarts do you give away?"

"And the Bergfelds weren't home."

"We could have them on cereal in the morning."

"So I wondered if ... "

"Anything, Mrs. Towson. I'd enjoy doing a favor for you. Especially after you did something like this for us."

"So I wondered if you would mind giving these strawberries to the Bergfelds."

"To the Bergfelds?"

"If you don't mind."

"Oh."

□

Everyone should be quick to listen, slow to speak.

JAMES 1:19

□

Questions for Family Discussion

Are you a good listener?

Do you interrupt when someone talks?

Have you ever gotten into trouble because you didn't hear everything that was said?

Do you say, "I know, I know" when someone is trying to explain things to you?

A GIFT OF STRAWBERRIES

51

A Cluttered Garage

MARK THREW his basketball across the garage. As it whistled past Clyde, the dog raised his head and rolled his eyes.

"Nobody has to clean up the garage but me. Just because I'm the oldest I have to do all the work around here."

With one hand he tossed his baseball bat in Claudia's direction. The gray cat bounded onto a shelf.

"You can see what's happening, can't you?" Mark directed his attention back to the long-eared dog. "Everybody else messed the place up and then I get stuck with cleaning it. Is that fair? I ask you, is that fair?"

Clyde stared.

Mark began collecting his fishing gear out of the corner. He placed his rod and reel in the wall cabinet. Disgusted, he dumped his tackle box inside and shoved the door closed.

"My friends are out playing ball. They are fishing and going to the park." He pointed his finger in Claudia's face as he raised his voice. "But here I'm doing everybody else's work. That's why parents have children, 'cause they can't get slaves."

Meet the Calderwoods

Claudia placed one paw over her left eye and barely stuck her tongue out.

"When I have kids, I'm going to tell them to go out and have a good time." Wheeling his bike to the back of the garage, he parked it against the wall. "I won't make them stay home and do everybody else's work. I'm almost a teenager.

"Your parents didn't make you work around the dog house, did they, Clyde? You bet not. Even dogs have a better life than I have."

Mark gathered four of his bike tires off the cement floor. One by one he hung the black circles on nails along the wall.

"You know what we need around here?" He stared directly into Claudia's whiskered face. "Kids need to go on strike. One Saturday all of us should sit down and refuse to work. That would bring the whole neighborhood to a standstill."

Slowly, Mark picked up his ball glove, football, and hockey stick.

"A guy gets tired of doing everybody else's work."

☐

Do everything without complaining.
PHIL. 2:14

☐

A CLUTTERED GARAGE   **163**

Questions for Family Discussion

How would you describe your attitude when your parents ask you to do something?

How often do you give your parents a pleasant answer when they tell you to do something?

Would someone describe you as a great complainer or a pleasant personality? Why?

52

The Lost Keys

D ID YOU BRING your purse along?" Mr. Calderwood asked his wife.

"Why, no. I left it back at the house."

"We might have some real problems. I dropped the car keys and I can't find them anywhere. I had them in my hand when I got out of the car. They must be on the ground someplace."

"It's hard to see on this gravel. There they are! Look, they are inside that drain." Mrs. Calderwood pointed.

"If I can lift this top off." Mr. Calderwood pulled at the iron grate. "It won't budge. We can see them but we can't reach them."

"Maybe this stick will do the job. I'll see if I can get it into the key ring." Mrs. Calderwood moved the stick around as she bent near the drain. "You had better give it a try, Mark."

"That's too bad. We can get the ring to stand up but it won't hook onto the end of the stick," Mr. Calderwood said as Mark worked over the drain.

"I've got an idea. Andy! Andy, come here," Mrs. Calderwood called.

THE LOST KEYS   **165**

"Do you think you can help?" she asked. "Our hands won't fit through the bars in the grate. Maybe your hands are small enough to reach the keys."

Andy bent down and tried to slide his fingers between the bars. His fingers fit fine but the wide part of his hand was too thick.

"Try over here," his father suggested. "The bars are a little farther apart."

Andy slipped his hand snugly between the bars, slid his fingers along the bottom of the drain, and clutched the keys. Carefully he pulled them out.

"Wow! Thanks!" Mr. Calderwood smiled as he rubbed his son's hands between his own. "I really thank God for you," Mr. Calderwood added as he wrapped one arm around Andy. "Not just now, but often I tell God just how glad I am that he gave you to us. I think God knows you need me and I need you. I really like you."

☐

I thank my God upon every remembrance of you.

PHIL. 1:3 KJV

☐

Questions for Family Discussion

Who do you thank God for?

Why do you thank God for them?

53

I'm a Star

THE MOUNTAIN STREAM rushed past their campsite. Mark and Sandra sat near the tent. Each wore a sweater to keep warm in the cool night air. As they rested on a fallen tree, Mark picked up stones and tossed them into the white rapids.

"Man, the sky is clear tonight," Sandra remarked.

"Sure can see a lot of stars." Mark threw a stone halfheartedly toward the heavens.

"Did you know there are a billion stars in our galaxy?" asked Sandra.

"No kidding," said Mark.

"And that's not all," she continued. "There may be one billion galaxies."

"Sounds like you passed science."

"I just mention it because I know you slept through that class."

"If you're going to give me a hard time, I'll dump you in the stream, Miss Know Everything."

"Stars are fireballs. They give off their own light," she persisted.

"That does it," Mark snarled. "One more fact and I'm out of here."

"Did you know that I'm a star?" asked Sandra.

"And all this time I thought you were a frog."

"Seriously. My Sunday school teacher told us we're all stars."

"Did she also say you're a pest?"

"She said that when Christians follow Christ without complaining, we shine like stars."

"You? You? You complain all the time," Mark objected.

"Not all the time," said Sandra emphatically.

"You complain almost all the time.

"Well, then, maybe I shine like a star the rest of the time."

"That's it. I'm out of here."

Mark headed for the tent.

□

Do everything without complaining or arguing, so that you may become blameless and pure, children of God without fault in a crooked and depraved generation, in which you shine like stars in the universe.
PHIL. 2:14–15

□

I'M A STAR

Questions for Family Discussion

Do you usually see the good or the bad around you?

At the supper table are you more likely to say good things or complain most of the time?

Do you shine like a star or rumble like a storm?

The Alley Cats

MARK LOOKED DOWN the alley to see what the noise was.

"There are a bunch of guys down there," Mark told his companion, Carlos, just as a brick thudded on the asphalt and then skidded toward their feet.

"They're throwing bricks at us," Carlos said as the two boys hurried to get out of the way.

When they were safely out of sight, Mark and Carlos peeked around the wall of the clothing store. They could see three boys about their age. Each was yelling and tossing bricks and cans and garbage along the alley.

"Look at those guys," Carlos whispered. "They're drinking. They're half out of their minds with booze."

"They're coming down the alley," said Mark. "Let's get out of here."

As Mark and Carlos started to leave, a police cruiser turned the corner and blocked the entrance to the alley. Quickly two police officers jumped from the car and grabbed the confused trio of drinkers.

"You boys are coming with us," one of the officers said. "Where do you live?"

"I live in a white house." The boy in the red windbreaker slurred his words as he spoke.

"Where did you guys get the beer?" The officer moved two of the boys toward the back of the police car.

"My brother gave it to me. But don't tell him I told you."

One boy stopped and threw up on the pavement.

The officers put all three of the drinkers firmly into the back seat of the cruiser. One officer radioed in some information to headquarters and soon they drove off with the bleary-eyed cargo.

"Those guys were sure out of it," Carlos said as he and Mark started walking down the street.

"I don't think any of them knew where they were or what they were doing." Mark kicked at a can on the sidewalk.

"I bet tomorrow morning their heads will be thumping like drums," Carlos added. "Let's hustle or we'll be late for the ball game."

☐

Similarly, encourage the young men to be self-controlled.

TITUS 2:6

☐

Meet the Calderwoods

Questions for Family Discussion

How are you a "too much" person? Do you play too much, tease too much, goof off too much, stay up late too much, swear too much, whine too much, or what?

What would you like to get better control over in your life?

How can you do it?

55

The George Washington Stare

RANDY EMPTIED his pockets as he looked for his flat whistle. He put first his comb, and then several coins and three baseball cards on the picnic table. Soon he fished out a small wad of dollar bills and one smooth stone, four jelly beans, and a dead bug.

"There it is," Randy said happily as he plunked down his flat blue whistle. "I knew I had it."

He picked it back up and blew into one end. A terrible, loud shriek pierced the air and Nathan, Kevin, Tony, and Andy each quickly covered his ears.

"Wow! Put that down," insisted Bob Watson, their Sunday school leader. "Let's get our fishing gear and head over to the lake."

The words had barely left his mouth when a gust of wind swept across the table. Baseball cards and dollar bills flew through the air and skipped across the grass.

"Hey!" Randy shouted. Everyone went diving for the tumbling pieces of paper.

"I've got two dollar bills," Kevin reported immediately.

"Here's your Kirby Puckett baseball card."

174   **Meet the Calderwoods**

In less than a minute the boys returned with what they had retrieved.

"Three dollar bills. I thought I had four."

"That's all we found," someone answered.

"I guess I was wrong." Randy thanked his friends.

The boys hurried to the lake and lined themselves along the bank, prepared their fishing rods, and baited their hooks. Tony was the first to cast out into the water.

"If anyone needs more salmon eggs, I've got plenty," volunteered Nathan.

As Andy baited his hook, he stopped to reach into his pocket and pull out a dollar bill. As he looked at the picture of George Washington, he was sure the president was staring at him. Andy stuffed it back into his pocket.

It's only a joke, he said to himself. *I'm going to give it back.*

Andy cast his rod out and watched his hook and anchor splash into the water.

Besides, he continued to think, *Randy doesn't even know how many dollars he had. He said so. What's the difference?*

Reeling his line in slowly Andy stopped and pulled the dollar bill back out. George Washington stared at him again. Quickly, Andy shoved the president deep into his pocket.

What if I hadn't picked it up? Andy argued with himself. *It would probably have rolled into the lake and no one would have it. Yeah, that's right.*

Besides, it's finders keepers, isn't it? Well, it ought to be. It really ought to be.

"Nuts," Andy said out loud as he laid his rod and reel on the ground.

Walking quietly over to where Randy stood fishing,

Andy reached into his pocket and pulled out the dollar bill.

"Any bites yet?" Andy asked.

"A couple," Randy answered without turning around.

Andy took one last look at the dollar bill and dropped it into Randy's bait box. As it floated down, Andy was almost sure he saw George Washington smile.

☐

He must return what he has stolen or taken by extortion, or what was entrusted to him, or the lost property he found.

LEV. 6:4

☐

Questions for Family Discussion

Is there something in your room that should be returned? Can you get that done today?

Why is it important to return it?

56

The Strange Disease

P ARKER'S DRIVE-IN was a busy place on a spring afternoon. As soon as school ended, a dozen or more children would walk or ride their bikes for ice cream or soft drinks.

Lisa liked to sit in one of the booths and eat a butterscotch Dilly Bar. She seldom sat alone. Today Micki joined her with a nutty cone.

"Too bad about Linda, huh?" Micki said as she bit into her ice cream.

"Too bad about what about Linda?" Lisa asked.

"You mean you haven't heard?"

"I never hear anything," Lisa replied.

"Well, it's all over school. Linda has filament."

"Filament?"

"Yeah, and it's pretty well advanced, too," Micki said with her mouth full.

"What will filament do?" Lisa wondered.

"They aren't sure, but she will probably have to go to the hospital."

"Can you get it from her?" Lisa asked.

"They say you can. It's best to stay away from her."

THE STRANGE DISEASE   **177**

"Where did you hear this?"

"Paula's uncle told her," Micki explained. "He said he saw a lot of it during the war."

"Man, that's too bad. Is it painful?" Lisa asked as she finished her Dilly Bar.

"You'd think so," Micki answered.

"Did you hear what Linda Bergren has?" Lisa asked her mother when she arrived home. "She has filament. And she is probably going to die from it."

"Never heard of it," said Mrs. Calderwood.

"It's real rare," Lisa continued. "Paula's uncle saw plenty of it during the war. Everyone is staying away from her."

"That's dreadful. Let's look it up." Mrs. Calderwood got the dictionary.

"Maybe they will put her in one of those bubbles," Lisa guessed. "She isn't supposed to touch anything."

"Did you say *filament?* According to the dictionary, if Linda has filament it simply means that she has hair. I think someone is kidding you guys." Mrs. Calderwood laughed. "I guess Paul's uncle did *see* a lot of filament during the war."

☐

But also gossips and busybodies, saying things they ought not to.
                                    1 TIM. 5:13

☐

Questions for Family Discussion

Why is gossiping wrong?

Imagine what it was like for Linda when all of her friends suddenly stopped spending time with her. How would you feel if people spread false stories about you?

What should Lisa have done when Micki told her the story about Linda?

57

Sneaking Out

T ALK TO DAD for me," Sandra said to her mother as they stood by the kitchen sink. "I've got to go to that party in the park."

"No thanks, Miss Calderwood," her mother said. She then turned to wipe off the stove. "You don't belong in a park at midnight without adult supervision."

"It's not what you think. They will just be listening to music and hanging out."

"Your friends can listen to music and hang out in our family room anytime you want." Mrs. Calderwood hung up her cloth.

"You act like we are going to drink or use drugs or something dumb like that. Parents always think the worst."

"Listen, lady, I don't know what you will be doing in the park and that's the point. And no other parent knows. You're better off without this one." Mrs. Calderwood left the kitchen.

Sandra fumed as she walked into the hall. She stopped by the back door. *Nobody's fair,* she thought. *Everybody treats me like a kid,* she told herself.

It was a big house, Sandra reasoned, and her parents were parked in front of the television. Silently she opened the closet door and took out her dark blue windbreaker. Just as carefully she opened the back door and dropped her jacket on the porch. She closed the door and remained inside. She wanted to think this one over.

"Sandra!" The ten-year-old jumped at the sound of her name. "Aren't you going to watch the movie with us? It's really funny." Mr. Calderwood hurried past her into the kitchen. He poured himself some diet pop and returned to the family room.

"I might later," Sandra answered feebly.

Carefully she put her right arm behind her and felt for the door knob. *Do it,* she told herself. *No one will know. They will think I went to bed. I do that a lot when I'm mad.*

So what if they do catch me? It's their fault. They should have let me go. She turned the knob slowly to make sure it didn't click.

I bet they snuck out when they were kids. Her mind was racing. Sandra could hear her parents laughing in the other room. She also felt her heart pounding.

It wouldn't be wrong to sneak out if you're being treated badly, she continued. Her hand felt wet on the door knob as she held it in a twisted position.

"Are you going to stand in the hall all night?" Her mother's head poked around. "You're missing the best part of the movie."

"I'll be right there." Sandra slowly released the door knob. She breathed a huge sigh of relief and headed for the family room.

□

No temptation has seized you except what is common to man. And God is faithful; he will not let you be tempted beyond what you can bear. But when you are tempted, he will also provide a way out so that you can stand up under it.

1 COR. 10:13

□

Questions for Family Discussion

Do you think Sandra's parents were fair?

How might Sandra have gotten her parents to understand better?

58

Cooling Down

COACH WANTS me to try the triple jump on Saturday," Pete told Mark as they jogged slowly around the track.

"I wish he'd let me do that instead of throwing the crummy shot put." Mark tightened the string on his sweatpants and re-tied it as he ran.

"One more lap and I'm heading in." Pete kicked his knees higher. "I'm really beat from running sprints."

"Look at Ted," Mark said. "He's sitting on the grass studying."

"Man, what a scuzz. Even my parents tell me to stay away from him," Pete spit out his words.

"There's nothing wrong with Ted." Mark reached down to touch his shoe tops as he jogged.

"You've got to be kidding. Look at that long hair and those worn out tennis shoes. I bet he got them at the Salvation Army."

"Nothing wrong with that," Mark replied. "At least he didn't steal them."

"You never know. Poor people will do anything. I just keep away from him."

"I'll tell you this, if you need a friend, Ted is hard to beat."

"I don't need a friend that badly," Pete shot back.

"You never know. If I have trouble with math, Ted's the first one I go to. He always understands the problem," Mark explained.

"Yeah, but just look at him. His jeans are worn out. And that shirt must be his dad's from the Vietnam War."

"Doesn't bother me. That just means he doesn't have any money." Mark stretched his arms over his head.

"That's the point, airhead. If you don't have money, there must be a reason like you're lazy or stupid or something."

"Maybe, and sometimes you get a few bad breaks."

"That's the point again. If you get bad breaks, it's because you're a klutz." The two boys stopped jogging and Pete leaned forward to stare into Mark's eyes.

"All I know is that he's a good guy. I never asked him where he got his tennis shoes," said Mark.

☐

He who mocks the poor shows contempt for their Maker.

PROV. 17:5

☐

Questions for Family Discussion

Is it hard to have friends who are different from us?

What did Pete say that was probably untrue?

Do you have friends whom no one else likes?

59

Hair Ball

WE SHOULD HAVE put Claudia in a box
with a lid," Lisa explained to her mother. "She is pacing
across the back seat."

"You're probably right. She is really afraid of the
vet." Mrs. Calderwood looked straight ahead as she
drove. "But Claudia doesn't care much for those hair
balls in her stomach either."

Claudia put her front paws on the car window as
she searched for a way to escape. Frustrated, the cat
returned to her restless pacing.

"She was hard enough to get into the car. I hope
she won't be hard to take out." Lisa reached back to
pet Claudia, but the cat would have none of it. "Boy, is
she mad."

As they drove into the parking lot at the veterinary
clinic, Claudia made one desperate leap, landing across
Lisa's shoulders.

The eight-year-old girl screamed.

Claudia clung tightly to Lisa's jacket.

"Don't panic," cautioned Mrs. Calderwood as she
turned off the engine. "She could scratch you. I'll hurry
around and open your door."

Carefully, Mrs. Calderwood let her daughter out of the car. Claudia's eyes remained wide as she traveled high above the ground toward the clinic door. Lisa's eyes were just as large as she worried what Claudia might do next.

Inside the clinic the receptionist rose quickly when she saw Lisa's unusual fur collar.

"Do you always dress this fancy?" she asked.

"Not really," was all Lisa could say.

"I take it your cat doesn't like haircuts," the receptionist said as she gently put her hands on Claudia.

"They're not her favorite activity," said Mrs. Calderwood.

"You must like your cat a lot to take good care of it."

Slowly, Claudia allowed the receptionist to pry each paw from the back of Lisa's neck. Lisa rubbed her stiff shoulders.

"We will take the same good care of your cat as you have," the receptionist assured them.

☐

A righteous man cares for the needs of his animal.

PROV. 12:10

☐

Questions for Family Discussion

Do you have any pets? What are their names?

How do you help take care of them?

What do you like about your pets?

Meet the Calderwoods

60

Noise at Midnight

SUDDENLY, ANDY sat straight up in bed.
He had to muffle his startled scream. Fortunately he
didn't awaken anyone, as far as he knew.

It must have been that crummy television show, he
told himself. Those creepy monsters and that dork with
the knife. That was why his parents didn't want him to
watch those shows, he recalled.

Andy snuggled back into the covers and sank his
head into the fluffy pillow. It would only take a few
minutes and he would be back to sleep, he reasoned.

KLUNK! KLUNK!

"What was that?" Andy whispered to himself. "It
sounds like chains dragging through the halls. Or is it
real or what?"

Andy pulled the pillow over his head, leaving just
enough room to peek out.

KLUNK! KLUNK!

It's in the hall, he thought. *I can't get out the
bedroom door and the windows are too high for an
escape.* Andy remained frozen to the mattress.

KLUNK! KLUNK!

Andy started to hum to himself quietly. Maybe everything would be all right if he could simply hum. Immediately a song from Sunday school came to mind.

"Hum . . . m . . . m. Hum . . . m . . . m . . . m. Doe Dee Da. Hum . . . m . . . m . . . m."

Andy couldn't remember all the words but he managed a few. Mostly he stuck to humming. Andy noticed that the noise had stopped, but he kept the music coming.

KLUNK! KLUNK! BUMP!

The door swung open and Andy sprang upright in bed. Through the doorway he saw Clyde, the family dog, walking slowly across the dark bedroom.

"It's just you," Andy said at the top of his voice. "Someone should take those dog tags off you."

Andy threw his pillow at Clyde, but not hard enough to hit him.

"Will you calm down in there?" Sandra called out.

Andy buried himself back in the covers. Feeling a bit foolish he began to hum again.

"Hum . . . m . . . m . . . m. Hum . . . m . . . m . . . m. Doe Dee Da."

☐

By day the LORD directs his love,
at night his song is with me—
a prayer to the God of my life.

PS. 42:8

☐

Questions for Family Discussion

Do you like to talk to God at night?

What do you sometimes talk about?